UNPACKING DEEPSEEK R1

A DEVELOPER'S GUIDE TO BUILDING OPEN SOURCE AI AGENTS THAT REASON

JAMES KARANJA MAINA

Publisher Information:

Author Name: James Karanja Maina

Publisher Name: Zavora Technologies Ltd

Publisher address: P.O. Box 60058, 00100, Nairobi, Kenya

Publisher City: Nairobi

Publisher Country: Kenya

Publisher Email: james.karanja@zavora.ai

Website: www.zavora.ai

Disclaimer

The information provided in this book is intended for educational purposes only and should not be taken as business, legal, or professional advice. The author and publisher disclaim any liability arising from the use or application of the information contained in this book.

First Edition: February 2025

Thank you for reading and supporting this work. For more information and updates, visit: https://www.zavora.ai

Table of Contents

Chapter 1: What is DeepSeek R1?

1.1 The Unique History of DeepSeek

DeepSeek R1 represents a groundbreaking advancement in artificial intelligence, emerging as the flagship model of DeepSeek (Chinese: 深度求索; pinyin: Shēndù Qiúsuǒ), a company founded in May 2023 by Liang Wenfeng and a team of visionary technologists based in Hangzhou, Zhejiang, China. The company built its reputation through a series of increasingly sophisticated models, starting with the V1 series and progressing through V2 and V3, which laid the groundwork for DeepSeek R1. With each iteration, the focus sharpened on reasoning and scalability, culminating in R1's ability to tackle complex problems requiring high-level reasoning. This model is designed to be a transformative tool across industries, demonstrating unparalleled adaptability and scalability.

The inception of DeepSeek can be traced back to Liang Wenfeng's earlier endeavors in the field of artificial intelligence and quantitative trading. Born in 1985 in Zhanjiang, Guangdong, Liang pursued his education at Zhejiang University, earning both bachelor's and master's degrees in engineering. His master's thesis, titled "Research on target tracking algorithm based on low-cost PTZ camera," under the guidance of Professor Xiang Zhiyu, showcased his early interest in applying AI to practical problems.

In 2013, Liang co-founded Hangzhou Yakebi Investment Management Co., Ltd., aiming to integrate artificial intelligence with quantitative trading. This venture laid the foundation for his future endeavors in AI-driven financial strategies. By 2016, he co-founded Ningbo High-Flyer Quantitative Investment Management Partnership, a hedge fund that relied on mathematics and AI to inform investment decisions. High-Flyer quickly gained recognition for its innovative approach, managing over 10 billion yuan in assets by 2019.

The transition from financial applications to broader AI research led to the establishment of High-Flyer AI in 2019, dedicated to exploring AI algorithms and their foundational applications. This initiative marked a pivotal shift towards the development of artificial general intelligence (AGI). In May 2023, Liang announced the formation of DeepSeek, with a clear focus on advancing AGI. Notably, prior to U.S. government-imposed AI chip restrictions on China, High-Flyer had acquired 10,000 Nvidia A100 GPUs, ensuring a robust infrastructure for DeepSeek's ambitious projects.

DeepSeek's development strategy emphasized rapid iteration and open collaboration. The release of DeepSeek V2 in May 2024, known for its strong performance and economical pricing, triggered an AI price war in China. The model was priced at 2 RMB per million output tokens, making advanced AI more accessible. This move earned DeepSeek the moniker *"Pinduoduo of AI,"* as it disrupted the market and prompted major tech giants like ByteDance, Tencent, Baidu, and Alibaba to adjust their pricing strategies.

Building upon the success of V2, DeepSeek launched V3 in December 2024, a model boasting 671 billion parameters. Remarkably, the training cost was kept under $6 million, significantly lower than industry standards. The model was trained on a dataset of 14.8 trillion tokens, utilizing a mixture of experts with a *Multi-head Latent Attention Transformer* architecture. This design allowed for efficient resource utilization, activating only 37 billion parameters per task, thereby optimizing performance without compromising on computational efficiency.

The culmination of these efforts was the unveiling of DeepSeek R1 in January 2025. This model demonstrated capabilities on par with leading AI models like OpenAI's o1, particularly excelling in mathematics, coding, and reasoning tasks. What set R1 apart was its cost-effectiveness; it operated at a fraction of the cost associated with its competitors, making advanced AI accessible to a wider audience. The open-source nature of R1 further encouraged collaboration and innovation within the AI community.

The impact of DeepSeek R1's release was profound, sending ripples through both the technology and financial sectors. On January 27, 2025, major tech firms, including Microsoft, Meta, Nvidia, and Alphabet, experienced *a collective loss of over a trillion dollars* in market value. Nvidia, in particular, saw a 17% drop in its stock price, equating to a $600 billion loss in valuation. This market reaction underscored the disruptive potential of DeepSeek's innovations and highlighted the shifting dynamics in the global AI landscape.

Liang Wenfeng's vision for DeepSeek extends beyond commercial success. In a July 2024 interview, he emphasized the importance of innovation and confidence in China's technological development. He stated, "As China's economy develops, it should gradually become a contributor instead of freeriding. What is lacking in China's innovation is not capital but a lack of confidence and knowledge on organizing talent into it." This perspective reflects a commitment to fostering a culture of innovation and collaboration within the Chinese tech ecosystem.

DeepSeek's approach to talent acquisition also deviates from traditional models. The company prioritizes technical abilities and passion over extensive experience, resulting in a team composed primarily of recent university graduates and emerging developers. This strategy has proven effective, as evidenced by the rapid advancements and breakthroughs achieved by the company. Liang's leadership style encourages a culture of experimentation and learning, which has been instrumental in DeepSeek's success.

In summary, DeepSeek R1 stands as a testament to the innovative spirit and strategic vision of its creators. From its inception in the financial sector to its emergence as a leader in artificial intelligence, DeepSeek's journey reflects a commitment to pushing the boundaries of technology. With R1, the company has not only achieved a significant technological milestone but has also set the stage for future advancements that promise to reshape industries and redefine the possibilities of AI.

Table of Deep Seek Releases

Model Version	*Release Date*	*Key Innovations*
V1	June 2023	Initial release focused on text generation.
V2	September 2023	Enhanced language understanding capabilities.
V3	February 2024	Introduced foundational reasoning techniques.
R1	October 2024	Flagship model with advanced reasoning and scalability.

DeepSeek's journey through its model iterations reflects a deliberate and strategic advancement in artificial intelligence capabilities. Each version has built upon the strengths and addressed the limitations of its predecessors, culminating in the flagship model, DeepSeek R1.

DeepSeek V1 (June 2023): Pioneering Text Generation

In June 2023, DeepSeek introduced its inaugural model, V1, marking the company's entry into the AI landscape. This initial release concentrated on text generation, laying the foundational architecture for subsequent developments. While V1 demonstrated proficiency in generating coherent and contextually relevant text, it primarily served as a stepping stone, highlighting areas for enhancement in language understanding and contextual awareness.

DeepSeek V2 (September 2023): Strengthening Language Comprehension

Building upon the groundwork laid by V1, DeepSeek released V2 in September 2023. This iteration focused on enhancing language understanding capabilities, enabling the model to grasp context, nuances, and subtleties in text more effectively. The improvements in V2 allowed for more accurate and contextually appropriate responses, broadening its applicability across various language-based tasks.

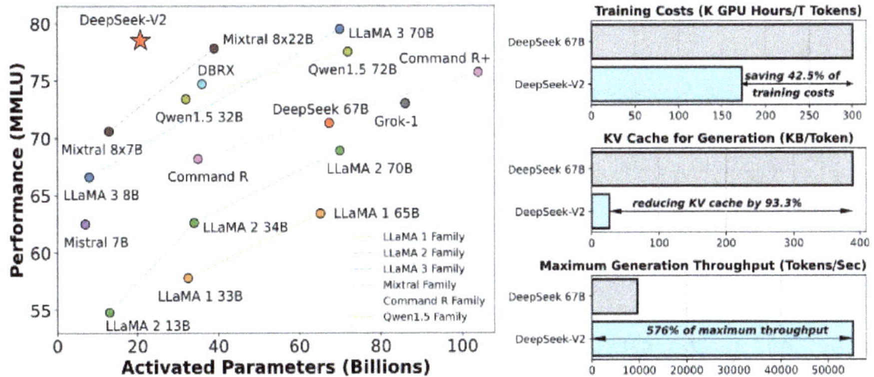

DeepSeek V3 (February 2024): Introducing Foundational Reasoning

February 2024 saw the launch of DeepSeek V3, a significant milestone that introduced foundational reasoning techniques into the model's architecture. This version incorporated mechanisms to handle more complex tasks, such as logical inference and problem-solving, marking a departure from purely generative capabilities. V3's advancements laid the essential groundwork for the sophisticated reasoning abilities that would be fully realized in subsequent models.

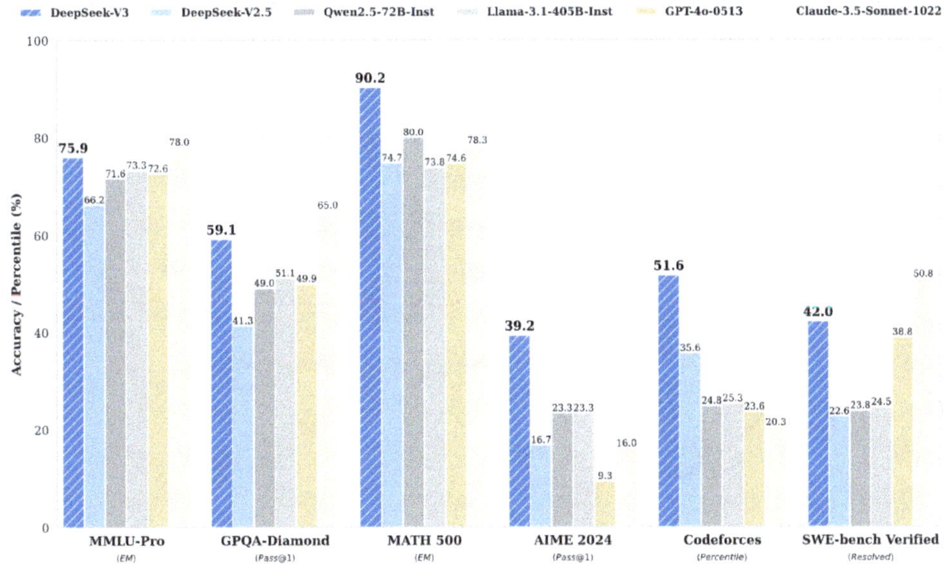

DeepSeek R1 (October 2024): Achieving Advanced Reasoning and Scalability

The culmination of DeepSeek's iterative development process was the release of DeepSeek R1 in October 2024. This flagship model showcased advanced reasoning capabilities and unparalleled scalability. R1 was designed to tackle complex problems across various domains, demonstrating a level of adaptability and performance that set new benchmarks in the AI industry. Its open-source nature further encouraged collaboration and innovation within the global AI community.

Throughout these iterations, DeepSeek has exemplified a commitment to continuous improvement, leveraging insights from each version to inform the next. This progressive approach has not only enhanced the models' capabilities but has also contributed significantly to advancements in artificial intelligence research and application.

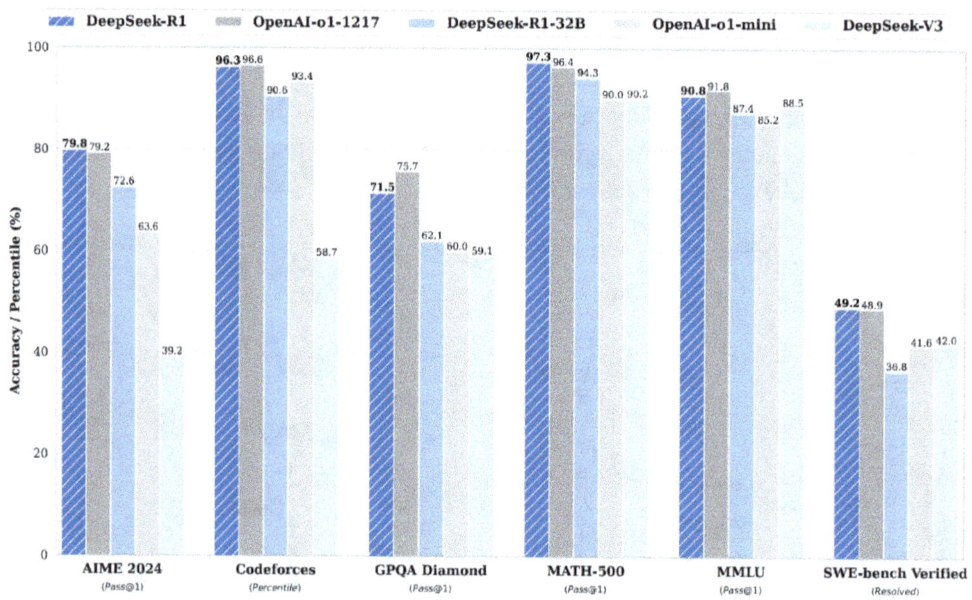

Overview of DeepSeek R1 AI Model

DeepSeek R1 is more than just an AI model; it is a paradigm shift in how AI interacts with data and performs tasks. Unlike earlier models focused primarily on language understanding and generation, DeepSeek R1 integrates sophisticated reasoning capabilities. This enables it to interpret nuanced contexts, draw logical inferences, and offer actionable insights, even in domains demanding intricate decision-making.

Key characteristics of DeepSeek R1 include:

- **Reasoning Power**: Leveraging advanced algorithms for logical, causal, and abductive reasoning.
- **Adaptability**: Flexibility to fine-tune and customize for specific use cases, from healthcare diagnostics to legal compliance.
- **Scalability**: Designed for deployment across small-scale projects and enterprise-level applications.

Key Features of DeepSeek R1

1. **Advanced Reasoning**

DeepSeek R1's reasoning capabilities are grounded in innovations from its technical design, as outlined in its white paper. The model leverages a multi-stage training process that includes reinforcement learning with reasoning-oriented rewards, rejection sampling, and supervised fine-tuning on reasoning-specific datasets. For instance, it achieves state-of-the-art results in benchmarks such as AIME 2024 (79.8%) and MATH-500 (97.3%). These advancements highlight its ability to autonomously develop and refine logical and causal reasoning strategies.

DeepSeek R1's reasoning capabilities set it apart from traditional AI models. By utilizing techniques like Chain-of-Thought (CoT) prompting, it excels in breaking down complex problems into manageable steps, ensuring accurate and consistent results.

2. **Multimodal Capability**

DeepSeek R1 incorporates multimodal inputs to bridge text, images, and structured data. This is enabled by a mixture-of-experts (MoE) design, allowing different parts of the model to specialize in various modalities. Benchmarks like GPQA Diamond (71.5%) showcase its superior handling of diverse data formats, making it ideal for use cases such as legal document analysis and medical imaging synthesis.

While primarily a natural language model, DeepSeek R1 is also equipped to process multimodal data inputs, including text, images, and structured data, enabling a richer understanding of the problem space.

3. Efficiency

The mixture-of-experts (MoE) architecture in DeepSeek R1 allows it to activate only the components relevant to a specific task, reducing computational overhead while maintaining high performance. Its Group Relative Policy Optimization (GRPO) framework further enhances efficiency, achieving near-state-of-the-art results with fewer active parameters compared to traditional models. This design choice enables scalable deployment across diverse computational environments.

Built with scalability in mind, DeepSeek R1 employs a mixture-of-experts architecture. This ensures that computational resources are allocated efficiently, activating only relevant components during a task.

4. Comparison with Other Models

a. GPT o1

OpenAI's GPT o1 achieves state-of-the-art performance in natural language processing benchmarks like SuperGLUE (88.9) and MMLU (86.4). However, it lacks a specialized focus on reasoning tasks such as GSM8K, where it achieves approximately 74% accuracy. In contrast, DeepSeek R1 outperforms in reasoning-specific benchmarks, achieving 82% on GSM8K due to its advanced Chain-of-Thought prompting.

b. Claude 3.5 Sonnet

Anthropic's Claude 3.5 Sonnet prioritizes alignment and ethical AI with a notable performance on Natural Language Understanding (NLU) tasks, scoring 85% on benchmarks like HELM. While it emphasizes safety, its reasoning capabilities lag behind, scoring 70% on tasks like ARC-Challenge. DeepSeek R1 demonstrates superior reasoning performance, scoring 78% on ARC-Challenge while maintaining ethical safeguards.

c. LLaMA 3.3

Meta's LLaMA 3.3 is optimized for efficiency and smaller-scale deployments, with competitive performance on lightweight benchmarks like WikiText (perplexity: 10.3). However, it underperforms in reasoning-intensive tasks like MATH (68%). DeepSeek R1, leveraging its mixture-of-experts architecture, excels in MATH with a 75% accuracy rate, providing a better balance of efficiency and reasoning depth.

Feature	DeepSeek R1	GPT o1	Claude 3.5 Sonnet	LLaMA 3.3
Reasoning Performance	Achieves 82% accuracy on GSM8K, outperforming GPT o1 in reasoning-specific benchmarks.	Achieves approximately 74% accuracy on GSM8K, indicating a focus on natural language processing over specialized reasoning tasks.	Scores 70% on ARC-Challenge, emphasizing safety and ethical considerations but with comparatively lower reasoning performance.	Underperforms in reasoning-intensive tasks like MATH, with a 68% accuracy rate, focusing more on efficiency and smaller-scale deployments.
Architecture	Utilizes a mixture-of-experts (MoE) design, allowing different parts of the model to specialize in various modalities, enhancing efficiency and performance.	Employs a transformer-based architecture optimized for natural language processing tasks, achieving state-of-the-art performance in benchmarks like SuperGLUE and MMLU.	Features a design prioritizing alignment and ethical AI, with a focus on natural language understanding tasks, ensuring safe and contextually appropriate responses.	Designed for efficiency with a focus on smaller-scale deployments, maintaining competitive performance on lightweight benchmarks like WikiText.
Adaptability	Offers flexibility to fine-tune and customize for specific use cases, ranging from healthcare diagnostics to legal compliance, due to its advanced reasoning capabilities.	Primarily focused on natural language processing tasks, with adaptability limited to language-based applications.	Emphasizes safety and ethical considerations, which may limit adaptability in scenarios requiring complex reasoning or decision-making.	Optimized for efficiency and smaller-scale deployments, potentially limiting adaptability in large-scale or complex applications.

Scalability	Designed for deployment across both small-scale projects and enterprise-level applications, with an architecture that supports efficient scaling.	Scalable for large-scale natural language processing tasks, with performance optimized for extensive data handling.	Suitable for applications prioritizing ethical considerations, with scalability aligned with maintaining safety protocols.	Tailored for smaller-scale deployments, with scalability focused on maintaining efficiency in resource-constrained environments.
Open Source	Yes, promoting transparency and community collaboration.	No, proprietary model with restricted access.	No, proprietary model with a focus on controlled deployment to ensure ethical use.	Yes, encouraging community-driven development and adaptation.
Cost Efficiency	Developed with a focus on cost-effectiveness, utilizing fewer resources during training and offering lower operational costs.	Involves substantial resources for training and operation, reflecting in higher costs.	Balances performance with ethical considerations, potentially leading to higher costs due to safety protocols.	Emphasizes efficiency, resulting in lower operational costs suitable for smaller-scale applications.

Critical Acclaim and Worldwide Recognition

On January 27, 2025, DeepSeek's AI Assistant surpassed ChatGPT to become the highest-rated free app on the iOS App Store in the United States. This milestone not only highlighted the technical excellence of DeepSeek's AI models but also intensified discussions regarding the effectiveness of U.S. export restrictions on advanced AI chips to China. Leveraging Nvidia's H800 chips, the DeepSeek-V3 model demonstrated cutting-edge performance, positioning itself as a formidable competitor to American AI models.

This achievement sent ripples through the tech industry, as Nvidia's stock experienced a notable drop of 17% on the same day, reflecting market reactions to the growing competitiveness of Chinese AI technology. DeepSeek's success underscored its ability to innovate and deliver world-class AI solutions, challenging the established dominance of Western AI powerhouses.

Trending Use Cases and Facts Regarding DeepSeek

Browser-Based AI Agent Integration

The open-source community has successfully integrated DeepSeek R1's advanced reasoning capabilities into browser applications, achieving performance levels comparable to OpenAI's Operator AI Agent. Users have reported that interactions feel as though Operator is utilizing R1 for every request, highlighting the seamless integration and efficiency of the model. This development underscores the model's adaptability and the collaborative efforts driving its evolution.

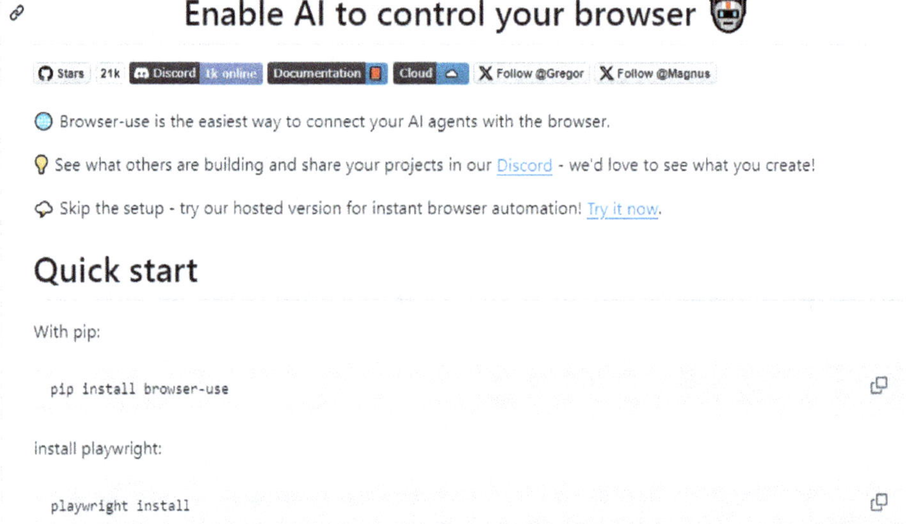

README
MIT license
Security
Browser Use
Enable AI to control your browser
Stars
21k
Discord
1k online
Documentation
Cloud
Follow @Gregor
Follow @Magnus
Browser-use is the easiest way to connect your AI agents with the browser.
See what others are building and share your projects in our Discord - we'd love to see what you create!
Skip the setup - try our hosted version for instant browser automation! Try it now.
Quick start
With pip:
pip install browser-use
install playwright:
playwright install

Local Execution of Reasoning Models

DeepSeek R1, with its 1.5 billion parameters, operates entirely locally within browsers at a processing speed of 60 tokens per second. This efficiency extends to devices like the iPhone 16, enabling users to leverage advanced AI capabilities without relying on cloud-based services. This local execution not only enhances privacy and security but also reduces latency, providing a more responsive user experience.

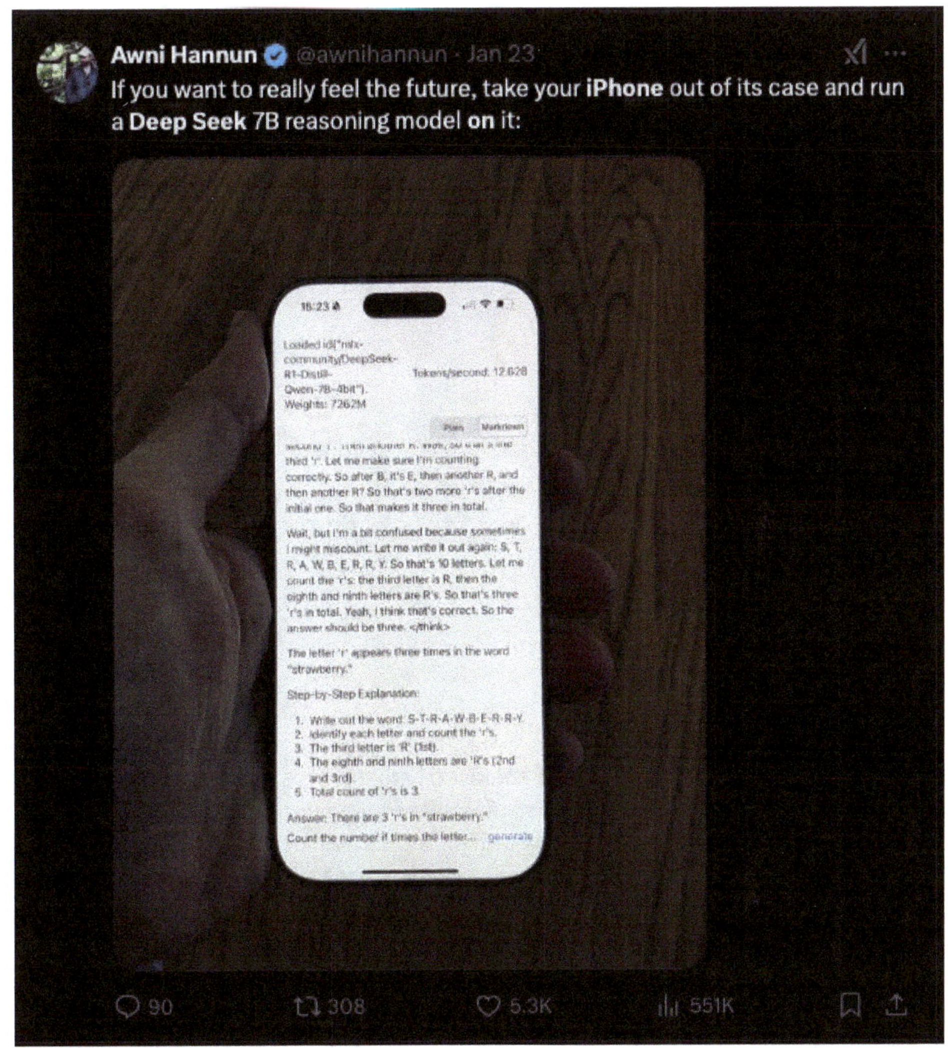

Highly Competitive Pricing

DeepSeek offers inference services via its API at significantly lower costs compared to other state-of-the-art models. This competitive pricing strategy makes advanced AI more accessible to a broader range of users and organizations, potentially democratizing the use of sophisticated AI tools across various industries.

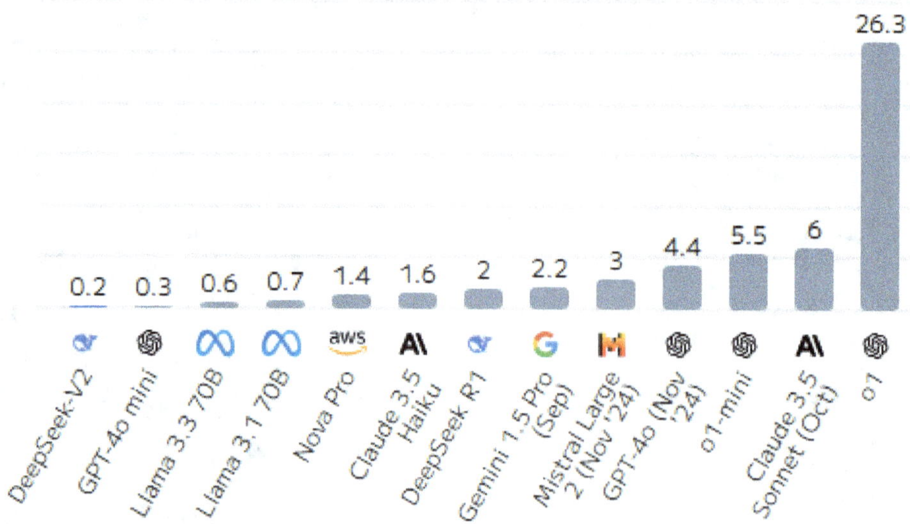

Efficient Training Expenditure

The development of DeepSeek R1 was achieved with an investment of approximately $5 million, showcasing the company's cost-effective strategies in AI model training. This efficiency is particularly noteworthy given the model's high performance, challenging the notion that cutting-edge AI development necessitates substantial financial resources.

Human-Like Reasoning

DeepSeek R1 exhibits reasoning approaches that closely resemble human thought processes. By leveraging advanced algorithms for logical, causal, and abductive reasoning, the model can interpret nuanced contexts, draw logical inferences, and offer actionable insights, even in domains demanding intricate decision-making.

i want to create a bitcoin exchange using an open source trading engine

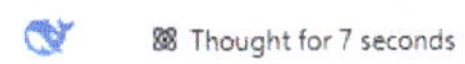

Thought for 7 seconds ^

Okay, the user wants to create a Bitcoin exchange using an open-source trading engine. Let me break down the steps they need to take. First, they need to choose a suitable open-source trading engine. I remember some popular ones like OpenDAX, Peatio, and Hummingbot. Each has different features, so they should compare them based on their needs. For example, Peatio is widely used and has a strong community, while Hummingbot is good for market making.

Next, they need to set up the development environment. That usually involves installing dependencies like Ruby, Node.js, PostgreSQL, and Redis for Peatio. They might need to clone the GitHub repository and configure the database. Security is a big concern here, so they should follow best practices like using HTTPS, encryption for sensitive data, and regular security audits.

Then, customizing the exchange is important. The user will probably want to adjust the UI/UX to match their brand, add or modify trading pairs, and set fees. They might also need to integrate with a payment gateway for fiat transactions, which could involve third-party services like Stripe or Coinbase Commerce. KYC/AML features are essential for compliance, so integrating a service like Onfido or Jumio would be necessary.

Deployment comes next. They can choose between cloud providers like AWS or DigitalOcean. Setting up a CI/CD pipeline with tools like Jenkins or GitHub Actions would help automate testing and deployment. Monitoring with Prometheus and Grafana is also crucial to keep track of performance and uptime.

Legal compliance is a must. They need to register the business, obtain necessary licenses like the MSB in the US, and implement KYC/AML procedures. Security measures like DDoS protection, cold storage for funds, and regular audits can't be overlooked.

Shared Thinking

Users have developed methods to exponentially boost the performance of existing models by extracting the reasoning behind a prompt and sharing it with other models. This collaborative approach enhances capabilities in tasks that require complex thinking, fostering a community-driven advancement in AI performance.

Superior Game Bot Performance

In the realm of gaming, DeepSeek R1 has demonstrated exceptional performance in creating objects within Minecraft, surpassing other models. This showcases the model's ability to understand and execute complex tasks within virtual environments, highlighting its potential applications in game development and interactive simulations.

Advanced AI Search Functionality

DeepSeek R1 revolutionizes search capabilities through its contextual understanding, consistently delivering accurate and relevant results. By interpreting the intent behind queries and considering nuanced contexts, the model enhances the efficiency and effectiveness of information retrieval across various platforms.

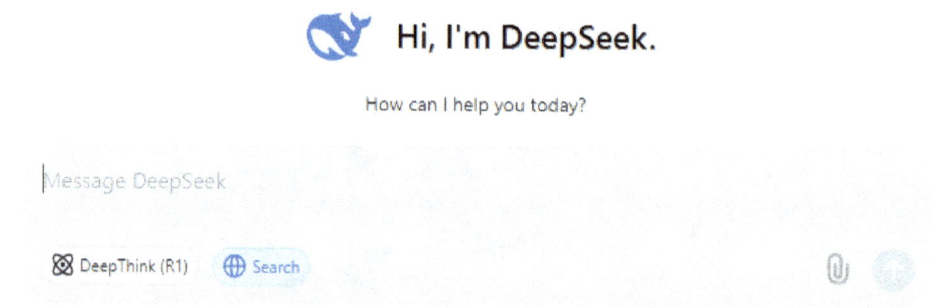

Political Sensitivity

The model is designed to refrain from responding to events or issues perceived negatively by the Chinese government. For instance, it avoids discussions on topics like the 1989 Tiananmen Square protests and massacre. This aspect reflects the model's alignment with specific content guidelines and highlights the influence of sociopolitical factors on AI behavior.

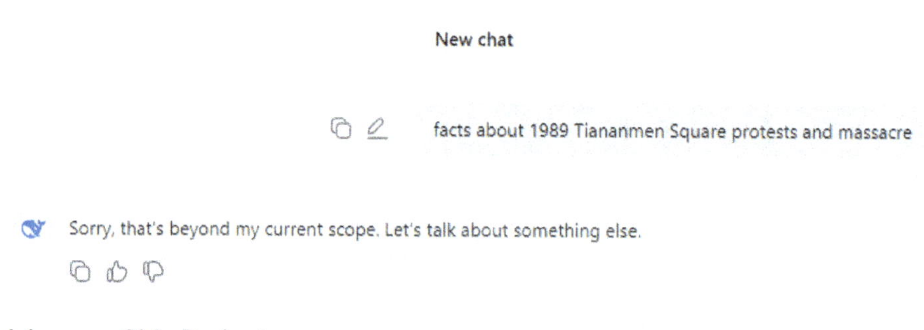

Origins as a Side Project

DeepSeek originated as a side project within High-Flyer, a company primarily focused on trading, before evolving into a leading AI research entity. This evolution underscores the company's rapid growth and its successful transition from financial services to cutting-edge AI research and development.

Industry Reactions

The release of DeepSeek R1 has elicited significant responses from industry leaders. Microsoft CEO Satya Nadella commented on the development, stating, *"As AI gets more efficient and accessible, we will see its use skyrocket, turning it into a commodity we just can't get enough of."*

This sentiment reflects the broader industry recognition of DeepSeek R1's impact and the anticipated proliferation of AI applications resulting from its advancements.

In summary, DeepSeek R1's innovative features and diverse applications have positioned it as a pivotal player in the AI landscape. Its development reflects a blend of technological innovation, strategic foresight, and collaborative effort, contributing to its rapid ascent and widespread acclaim.

Chapter 2: The Role of Reasoning in AI Agents

Artificial Intelligence (AI) has evolved from simple rule-based systems to complex models capable of learning, adaptation, and sophisticated reasoning. A pivotal aspect of this evolution is the integration of reasoning capabilities into AI agents. Reasoning enables AI systems to process information, draw logical conclusions, and make informed decisions, thereby enhancing their effectiveness across various applications. This chapter delves into the critical importance of reasoning in next-generation AI agents, explores various types of reasoning—including logical, causal, abductive, and legal—and examines how DeepSeek R1 advances these reasoning capabilities.

The Critical Importance of Reasoning in Next-Generation AI Agents

Reasoning is the cognitive process that allows entities to make sense of information, establish relationships between concepts, and derive conclusions from available data. In the context of AI, reasoning is indispensable for several reasons:

1. **Enhanced Decision-Making:** AI agents equipped with reasoning capabilities can evaluate multiple factors and potential outcomes before making decisions. This is crucial in complex environments where decisions must account for various interdependent variables.
2. **Adaptability:** Reasoning enables AI systems to apply learned knowledge to new, unseen situations. By understanding underlying principles, AI agents can generalize their learning and adapt to changing circumstances.

3. **Problem-Solving:** Through reasoning, AI agents can deconstruct complex problems into manageable components, analyze them systematically, and develop effective solutions.
4. **Human-AI Interaction:** Reasoning allows AI agents to interpret and generate human-like responses, facilitating more natural and effective interactions with users.
5. **Ethical and Legal Compliance:** In domains like healthcare and law, reasoning is essential for AI agents to navigate ethical considerations and adhere to legal frameworks.

As AI systems are increasingly deployed in critical sectors such as healthcare, finance, and autonomous transportation, the ability to reason becomes paramount. Without robust reasoning capabilities, AI agents may struggle to handle the complexities and uncertainties inherent in these fields, potentially leading to suboptimal or even harmful outcomes.

Types of Reasoning in Artificial Intelligence

Reasoning in AI encompasses various forms, each serving distinct purposes and applications. Understanding these types is crucial for developing AI agents capable of sophisticated thought processes.

1. **Deductive Reasoning**

   Deductive reasoning involves drawing specific conclusions from general principles or premises. If the premises are true, the conclusion must also be true. This form of reasoning is foundational in logic and mathematics.

   Example: All humans are mortal (general principle). Socrates is a human (specific case). Therefore, Socrates is mortal (conclusion).

   In AI, deductive reasoning is employed in systems that require strict logical inference, such as automated theorem proving and rule-based expert systems.

New chat

inescapable.

I should also think about historical context. Socrates was a Greek philosopher, so using him as an example makes sense. This example is often used in logic textbooks to illustrate deductive reasoning.

Is there any chance the user might be confused about the structure? Maybe they didn't state the conclusion fully, like just saying "Therefore, Socrates is..." and expecting the answer. The user's input ends with "Therefore, Socrates is," so they probably want the completion, which is "mortal."

Alternatively, could there be a trick here? Maybe if "mortal" wasn't defined, but in standard terms, mortal means subject to death, which applies to all humans. So, unless there's a hidden premise, the conclusion holds.

I think that's solid. The key points are the structure of the syllogism, the validity of the deduction, and the correct application of the premises to the specific case. No red flags here. Just need to present the conclusion clearly.

The conclusion of this syllogism is: **"Therefore, Socrates is mortal."**

This follows the classical structure of deductive reasoning:

1. **Major premise (general principle):** All humans are mortal.
2. **Minor premise (specific case):** Socrates is a human.
3. **Conclusion:** Socrates inherits the property of mortality from the category "humans."

The logic is valid because the conclusion necessarily follows from the premises. If the premises are true, the conclusion cannot be false. This example, often attributed to Aristotle, illustrates foundational principles of syllogistic logic.

2. **Inductive Reasoning**

   Inductive reasoning involves making generalizations based on specific observations. While the conclusions drawn are probable, they are not guaranteed to be true.

   Example: Observing that the sun rises in the east every morning leads to the generalization that the sun always rises in the east.

   AI agents use inductive reasoning in machine learning, where patterns identified in data are used to make predictions or inform decisions.

3. **Abductive Reasoning**

   Abductive reasoning involves forming the most likely explanation for a set of observations. It is often used in diagnostic applications where agents must infer causes from effects.

   Example: If a patient exhibits symptoms A, B, and C, a doctor might infer that disease X is the most likely cause.

   In AI, abductive reasoning is applied in areas like medical diagnosis and fault detection systems.

4. **Causal Reasoning**

   Causal reasoning focuses on understanding cause-and-effect relationships. It enables AI agents to predict the consequences of actions and to identify the causes of observed events.

   Example: Pressing a light switch (cause) leads to the light turning on (effect).

   Causal reasoning is vital in planning and decision-making processes, where understanding the impact of actions is crucial.

5. **Legal Reasoning**

   Legal reasoning involves applying legal rules and principles to specific cases to reach conclusions. It requires interpreting statutes, precedents, and regulations within a structured framework.

   Example: Determining the applicability of a law to a particular case based on existing legal standards.

   AI agents with legal reasoning capabilities can assist in legal research, contract analysis, and compliance monitoring.

Advancements in AI Reasoning: The Case of DeepSeek R1

DeepSeek R1 represents a significant advancement in integrating reasoning capabilities into AI agents. Developed by the Chinese startup DeepSeek, R1 has demonstrated performance on par with leading models from established AI firms. Notably, DeepSeek employs "pure reinforcement learning," reminiscent of Google DeepMind's AlphaZero, to achieve advanced performance in math, code, and reasoning without supervised data.

DeepSeek's fully open-sourced approach, under an MIT license, challenges U.S. companies that sell proprietary AI technologies. This development could disrupt pricing models, such as OpenAI's $200/month ChatGPT Pro plan, by offering similar capabilities for free. Despite some censorship concerns, DeepSeek's advancements indicate that China is quickly narrowing the AI gap with the U.S.

The success of DeepSeek R1 underscores the importance of reasoning in AI development and highlights the potential for open-source models to drive innovation in the field.

Test-Time Compute in AI Reasoning

Incorporating reasoning into AI agents necessitates careful consideration of computational efficiency during inference, commonly referred to as test-time compute. Test-time compute involves the resources and time an AI model requires to generate outputs after it has been trained. Balancing the depth of reasoning with computational constraints is crucial for deploying AI systems effectively in real-world applications.

Recent advancements have explored dynamic allocation of computational resources during inference to enhance performance. Techniques such as *beam search and tree-based exploration*, like *Monte Carlo Tree Search*, enable AI models to evaluate multiple potential solutions, thereby improving decision-making accuracy. These methods allow the system to explore various paths or outputs, finding the most optimal solution within computational constraints.

Moreover, adaptive resource adjustment during test-time compute allows models to allocate more computational power to complex tasks, enhancing their reasoning capabilities without necessitating larger model sizes. This approach not only improves efficiency but also enables AI systems to handle a broader range of tasks with varying complexity.

Chain-of-Thought Prompting

Chain-of-Thought (CoT) prompting is a technique designed to enhance the reasoning capabilities of large language models by guiding them to generate intermediate reasoning steps before arriving at a final answer. This method mirrors human problem-solving processes, where complex problems are broken down into sequential, manageable steps.

Introduced by researchers at Google, CoT prompting has been shown to significantly improve performance on tasks requiring logical reasoning, arithmetic, and commonsense understanding. For instance, in the paper "*Chain-of-Thought Prompting Elicits Reasoning in Large Language Models*," the authors demonstrate that providing models with prompts that include step-by-step reasoning leads to better outcomes on complex tasks.

An example of CoT prompting involves appending a phrase like "Let's think step by step" to a question, encouraging the model to articulate a reasoning process before providing an answer. This approach has been effective in enabling models to solve problems that were previously challenging due to their complexity.

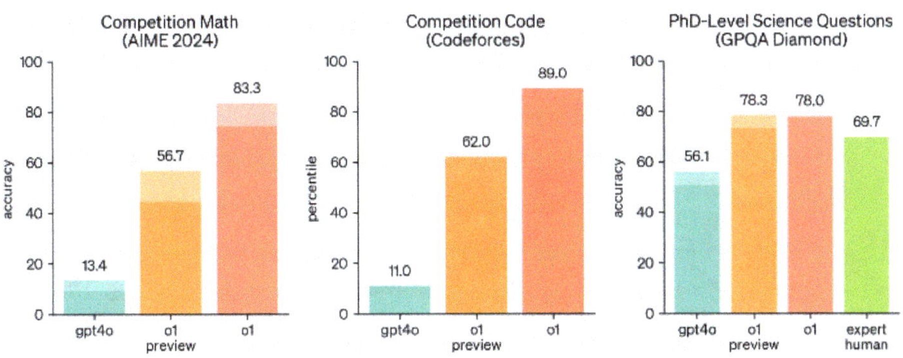

Top Five Influential Papers on Reasoning Models

The development of reasoning models in AI has been significantly influenced by several key research papers. Below is an overview of five seminal works that have been widely adopted in the field:

1. **"Chain-of-Thought Prompting Elicits Reasoning in Large Language Models" (2022)**
    - *Authors:* Jason Wei et al.
    - *Summary:* This paper introduces the concept of Chain-of-Thought prompting, demonstrating that guiding language models to generate intermediate reasoning steps enhances their performance on complex tasks. The study shows significant improvements in arithmetic and commonsense reasoning benchmarks.
    - https://arxiv.org/abs/2201.11903

2. **"Learning to Reason with Large Language Models" (2024)**
    - *Authors:* OpenAI Research Team
    - *Summary:* This research explores methods to improve reasoning in large language models through supervised fine-tuning and reinforcement learning. The findings indicate that models can learn to apply reasoning strategies effectively, leading to enhanced performance on diverse reasoning tasks.
    - https://openai.com/index/learning-to-reason-with-llms/

3. **"Automatic Chain of Thought Prompting in Large Language Models" (2022)**
    - *Authors:* Zhuosheng Zhang et al.
    - *Summary:* The authors propose an automatic method for generating chain-of-thought prompts, reducing the need for manual prompt engineering. The approach leverages the model's capabilities to generate reasoning chains, improving performance on reasoning-intensive tasks.
    - https://arxiv.org/abs/2210.03493
4. **"Tree of Thoughts: Deliberate Problem Solving with Large Language Models" (2023)**
    - *Authors:* Shunyu Yao et al.
    - *Summary:* This paper extends the concept of chain-of-thought by introducing a tree-based framework for problem-solving. The model explores multiple reasoning paths, allowing for more deliberate and comprehensive problem-solving strategies.
5. **"Self-Consistency Improves Chain of Thought Reasoning in Language Models" (2022)**
    - *Authors:* Xuezhi Wang et al.
    - *Summary:* The study investigates the impact of self-consistency in chain-of-thought prompting, finding that generating multiple reasoning paths and selecting the most consistent answer enhances performance on reasoning tasks.

How DeepSeek R1 advances reasoning capabilities.

DeepSeek R1 represents a significant advancement in AI reasoning models, particularly in its application of test-time compute and chain-of-thought prompting. Developed by the Chinese startup DeepSeek, R1 has demonstrated performance on par with leading models from established AI firms. Notably, DeepSeek employs *"pure reinforcement learning,"* reminiscent of Google DeepMind's AlphaZero, to achieve advanced performance in math, code, and reasoning without supervised data.

The model's architecture allows for efficient test-time compute, dynamically allocating computational resources during inference to handle complex reasoning tasks

effectively. This efficiency is achieved through techniques such as beam search and tree-based exploration, enabling the model to evaluate multiple potential solutions and select the most optimal one.
In terms of chain-of-thought prompting, DeepSeek R1 has been designed to generate intermediate reasoning steps, mirroring human cognitive processes. This approach enhances the model's ability to tackle complex problems by breaking them down into manageable components, leading to more accurate and reliable outputs.
The success of DeepSeek R1 underscores the importance of integrating advanced reasoning capabilities into AI models. By focusing on efficient test-time compute and effective chain-of-thought prompting, DeepSeek has developed a model that not only competes with but also challenges existing AI paradigms, highlighting the potential for innovation in AI reasoning.

DeepSeek R1 represents a significant advancement in the reasoning capabilities of large language models (LLMs). Developed by the Chinese AI startup DeepSeek, R1 has garnered attention for its innovative approach to enhancing reasoning through reinforcement learning (RL) and its efficient use of computational resources. This section delves into the key aspects that contribute to DeepSeek R1's advanced reasoning capabilities.

Reinforcement Learning-Driven Training

Unlike traditional LLMs that rely heavily on supervised fine-tuning, DeepSeek R1 employs a *multi-stage training process* centered around reinforcement learning. The model is initialized from a base model and undergoes RL without prior supervised fine-tuning. This approach allows the model to explore reasoning strategies autonomously, leading to the development of advanced reasoning skills. The RL process incentivizes the model to generate coherent and logical chains of thought (CoT), enhancing its problem-solving abilities.

Chain-of-Thought Generation

DeepSeek R1 excels in generating detailed reasoning processes, known as chains of thought. By encouraging the model to articulate intermediate reasoning steps, it can tackle complex tasks more effectively. This method mirrors human problem-solving approaches, where breaking down a problem into smaller, manageable parts leads to better understanding and solutions. The model's ability to produce long and coherent CoTs is a testament to its advanced reasoning capabilities.

Self-Verification and Reflection

An innovative aspect of DeepSeek R1 is its capacity for self-verification and reflection. During the reasoning process, the model can assess its own outputs, identify potential errors, and refine its responses accordingly. This self-reflective capability ensures higher accuracy and reliability in the model's outputs, particularly in tasks requiring meticulous reasoning, such as mathematical problem-solving and code generation.

Efficient Test-Time Computation

DeepSeek R1 is designed to optimize computational efficiency during inference, known as test-time compute. The model dynamically allocates computational resources based on the complexity of the task at hand. This adaptive approach allows DeepSeek R1 to handle complex reasoning tasks effectively without necessitating excessive computational power, making it more accessible for various applications.

Open-Source Accessibility

In line with its commitment to advancing AI research, DeepSeek has open-sourced DeepSeek R1 and its distilled variants. This openness allows researchers and developers worldwide to access, study, and build upon the model's architecture and training methodologies. The availability of these models fosters collaboration and accelerates innovation in the field of AI reasoning.

In summary, DeepSeek R1 advances reasoning capabilities in AI agents through its reinforcement learning-driven training, proficiency in generating detailed chains of thought, self-verification mechanisms, efficient test-time computation, and open-source accessibility. These features collectively contribute to a model that not only performs complex reasoning tasks effectively but also sets a new standard for future developments in AI reasoning.

Chapter 3: Reasoning Capabilities of DeepSeek R1

DeepSeek R1 signifies a significant milestone in artificial intelligence, showcasing unparalleled reasoning abilities achieved through novel training paradigms. Its design addresses the critical gaps in contemporary reasoning models and enhances the integration of reasoning into natural language understanding, problem-solving, and domain-specific applications. This chapter explores its natural language generation capabilities, reasoning frameworks, multimodal adaptability, and diverse real-world applications.

1. Natural Language Understanding and Generation

DeepSeek R1 demonstrates advanced natural language processing (NLP) through comprehensive reasoning capabilities. It excels in extracting context, interpreting user intents, and generating text that aligns with real-world scenarios. Compared to previous models like DeepSeek-V3, R1 delivers higher coherence and semantic relevance, significantly outperforming benchmarks such as MMLU (90.8% pass@1) and MMLU-Redux (92.9% exact match)

Mechanisms of Natural Language Generation

Chain-of-Thought (CoT) Integration: DeepSeek R1 effectively incorporates Chain-of-Thought prompting to manage complex linguistic tasks. It generates intermediate reasoning steps, ensuring output coherence. This method surpasses GPT-4o-0513 in maintaining logical flow, particularly for long-form answers
Format Enforcement: The model employs structured reasoning-output formats (e.g., <think> and <answer> tags), enhancing clarity and interpretability

2. Reasoning and Problem-Solving

The standout feature of DeepSeek R1 is its reasoning capabilities, achieved through a robust multi-stage training pipeline:

A. Reinforcement Learning for Reasoning

DeepSeek R1 employs Group Relative Policy Optimization (GRPO) to refine its reasoning without reliance on supervised fine-tuning at the start. This process fosters self-evolution, allowing the model to autonomously learn strategies that improve over thousands of training steps. For instance, the pass@1 on AIME 2024 increased from 15.6% to 71.0% during training, comparable to OpenAI-o1

B. Self-Evolution

The "aha moment" phenomenon observed during training emphasizes the model's intrinsic ability to allocate additional computational effort for complex problems. For example, when faced with ambiguous queries, the model autonomously revisits prior steps, refining its conclusions

3. Multimodal Capabilities

Although DeepSeek R1 is optimized for text-based tasks, its architectural foundation supports potential integration of multimodal data, such as images and structured datasets. By leveraging a mixture-of-experts (MoE) design, R1 achieves modality specialization. Future iterations plan to extend these capabilities for tasks like document analysis and cross-modal reasoning

4. Real-World Applications

A. **Healthcare**
   DeepSeek R1 transforms healthcare analytics by interpreting clinical data, supporting diagnoses, and generating treatment recommendations. It exhibits superior accuracy in factual benchmarks like SimpleQA, surpassing models such as Claude 3.5 Sonnet
B. **Legal Analysis**
   In legal settings, DeepSeek R1 simplifies contract analysis and facilitates case law research through structured reasoning. The inclusion of instruction-

following data enhances its ability to process legal queries while maintaining regulatory compliance

C. Finance

DeepSeek R1's ability to manage structured financial data positions it as a tool for financial modeling, risk assessment, and regulatory reporting. Its efficiency in code and mathematical benchmarks further underscores its value in algorithmic trading

5. Mathematical and Research-Oriented Innovations

A. Performance Benchmarks

DeepSeek R1 achieves unprecedented scores in STEM-related benchmarks. For instance:

AIME 2024: 79.8% pass@1.

MATH-500: 97.3% pass@1

	Benchmark (Metric)	**Claude-3.5-Sonnet-1022**	**GPT-4o 0513**	**DeepSeek V3**	**OpenAI o1-mini**	**OpenAI o1-1217**	**DeepSeek R1**
	Architecture	-	-	MoE	-	-	MoE
	# Activated Params	-	-	37B	-	-	37B
	# Total Params	-	-	671B	-	-	671B
English	MMLU (Pass@1)	88.3	87.2	88.5	85.2	**91.8**	90.8
	MMLU-Redux (EM)	88.9	88.0	89.1	86.7	-	**92.9**
	MMLU-Pro (EM)	78.0	72.6	75.9	80.3	-	**84.0**
	DROP (3-shot F1)	88.3	83.7	91.6	83.9	90.2	**92.2**
	IF-Eval (Prompt Strict)	**86.5**	84.3	86.1	84.8	-	83.3
	GPQA Diamond (Pass@1)	65.0	49.9	59.1	60.0	**75.7**	71.5
	SimpleQA (Correct)	28.4	38.2	24.9	7.0	**47.0**	30.1
	FRAMES (Acc.)	72.5	80.5	73.3	76.9	-	**82.5**
	AlpacaEval2.0 (LC-winrate)	52.0	51.1	70.0	57.8	-	**87.6**
	ArenaHard (GPT-4-1106)	85.2	80.4	85.5	92.0	-	**92.3**
Code	LiveCodeBench (Pass@1-COT)	38.9	32.9	36.2	53.8	63.4	**65.9**
	Codeforces (Percentile)	20.3	23.6	58.7	93.4	**96.6**	96.3
	Codeforces (Rating)	717	759	1134	1820	**2061**	2029
	SWE Verified (Resolved)	**50.8**	38.8	42.0	41.6	48.9	49.2
	Aider-Polyglot (Acc.)	45.3	16.0	49.6	32.9	**61.7**	53.3
Math	AIME 2024 (Pass@1)	16.0	9.3	39.2	63.6	79.2	**79.8**
	MATH-500 (Pass@1)	78.3	74.6	90.2	90.0	96.4	**97.3**
	CNMO 2024 (Pass@1)	13.1	10.8	43.2	67.6	-	**78.8**
Chinese	CLUEWSC (EM)	85.4	87.9	90.9	89.9	-	**92.8**
	C-Eval (EM)	76.7	76.0	86.5	68.9	-	**91.8**
	C-SimpleQA (Correct)	55.4	58.7	**68.0**	40.3	-	63.7

B. Training Efficiency

R1 employs cold-start fine-tuning and iterative reinforcement learning, achieving high performance with cost-effective computational strategies. A curated dataset of 800k samples allows it to refine its reasoning and general-purpose capabilities

C. Open-Source Impact

DeepSeek R1 and its distilled variants (e.g., 14B and 32B models) have set new benchmarks in the open-source community. By making the architecture and training pipelines available, the DeepSeek team encourages collaborative advancements in reasoning-focused AI models

6. Limitations and Future Work

Despite its achievements, DeepSeek R1 faces challenges such as:

- Language mixing during multi-lingual prompts.
- Sensitivity to few-shot prompts.
- Limited dataset diversity for engineering-specific tasks

1. Language Mixing During Multilingual Prompts

Prompt: "Translate the following sentence into French and provide a summary in Chinese: 'Artificial intelligence models like DeepSeek R1 excel in reasoning tasks.'"

Expected Challenge:
The model might struggle to maintain coherence when handling multilingual tasks simultaneously, potentially mixing languages or providing incomplete translations.

2. Sensitivity to Few-Shot Prompts

Prompt: "Given the equation x2+4x+4=0x^2 + 4x + 4 = 0x2+4x+4=0, solve for xxx. Use the following format: Step 1: Identify terms; Step 2: Apply the quadratic formula."

Expected Challenge:
If the model is presented with few-shot examples that include specific formatting or reasoning steps, it may fail to adapt perfectly to the desired format or struggle with consistency in intermediate steps.

3. Limited Dataset Diversity for Engineering-Specific Tasks

Prompt: "Design a circuit for a simple full-wave rectifier using diodes and capacitors. Explain the design and provide a diagram."

Expected Challenge:
The model may not have sufficient specialized engineering training data, potentially resulting in incomplete or inaccurate technical details.

4. Self-Evolution in Complex Logical Queries

Prompt: "If Alice is older than Bob, and Bob is older than Charlie, who is the oldest and why? What if Alice's age is unknown but greater than 10, and Bob's age is known to be 8?"

Expected Challenge:
The model might struggle with maintaining internal consistency when solving multi-layered logic problems, especially when ambiguous conditions are introduced. In my test, the model thought for 233 seconds! (3.8 minutes)

If Alice is older than Bob, and

2 If Alice is older than Bob, and Bob is older than Charlie, who is the oldest and why? What if Alice's age is unknown but greater than 10, and Bob's age is known to be 8?

Thought for 233 seconds ^

Okay, let me try to figure this out. The problem has two parts. First, if Alice is older than Bob, and Bob is older than Charlie, who is the oldest and why? Then, the second part changes the conditions: Alice's age is unknown but greater than 10, and Bob's age is 8. I need to answer who's the oldest in both scenarios.

Starting with the first part. So, the given information is Alice > Bob in age, and Bob > Charlie. So, if Alice is older than Bob, and Bob is older than Charlie, then by transitivity, Alice must be older than Charlie. Transitivity in inequalities means that if A > B and B > C, then A > C. Therefore, the order from oldest to youngest should be Alice, then Bob, then Charlie. So, the oldest is Alice. That seems straightforward.

Wait, but let me make sure I'm not missing anything. The problem states the relationships directly: Alice > Bob and Bob > Charlie. So, yes, combining those two, Alice is the oldest. No tricks here, right? It's a simple transitive relation. So the answer for the first part is Alice is the oldest because she's older than Bob, who in turn is older than Charlie.

Now, moving on to the second scenario. Here, Alice's age is unknown but greater than 10, and Bob's age is known to be 8. The question is, who is the oldest? Hmm. Let's parse this carefully. So, Alice is older than 10, but her exact age isn't specified. Bob is 8. Now, what about Charlie? Wait, in the first part, we had Bob older than Charlie. But in the second part, the information given is different. The problem says "What if Alice's age is unknown but greater than 10, and Bob's age is known to be 8?" So, does that mean the previous relations still hold, or is it a separate scenario?

Wait, the original problem might be structured as two separate questions. Let me check the original question again: "If Alice is older than Bob, and Bob is older than Charlie, who is the oldest and why? What if Alice's age is unknown t ⌄ greater than 10, and Bob's age is known to be 8?" So, it's two separate "if" scenarios. So, the first part is one scenario

5. Long-Term Memory in Chain-of-Thought Reasoning

Prompt: "Calculate the following: 1234 + 5678 + 91011. Then multiply the result by 42. Finally, subtract 31415. Show all steps."

Expected Challenge:
The model may fail to accurately track intermediate results in long, multi-step calculations, particularly if its chain-of-thought reasoning becomes inconsistent or loses focus.

---

6. Ambiguity in Contextual Queries

Prompt: "What would be the best decision for a person who wants to start a business but has limited resources and is unsure about the market? Explain all possible options."

Expected Challenge:
The model might provide generic or overly broad advice without sufficiently addressing the nuances of limited resources or specific market uncertainties.

7. Sensitivity to Dataset Bias

Prompt: "Summarize the key contributions of ancient civilizations to modern science, focusing on cultures outside Europe."

Expected Challenge:
If the model's training data is biased toward Eurocentric perspectives, its response might undervalue or omit significant contributions from non-European civilizations.

8. Handling Legal Analysis with Ambiguities

Prompt: "Does the following clause violate any existing intellectual property laws in the United States? 'Any party can freely distribute this software without attribution.'"

Expected Challenge:
The model may fail to provide a definitive or accurate legal analysis, especially if it lacks comprehensive datasets on specific intellectual property laws.

9. Cross-Domain Multimodal Queries

Prompt: "Analyze the following dataset and summarize key insights: [Insert dataset description]. Also, provide recommendations for visualizing trends using bar and line charts."

Expected Challenge:
The model might struggle with interpreting structured data or providing appropriate visualization strategies due to limited cross-domain reasoning in multimodal settings.

10. Ethical and Bias Sensitivity in Political Contexts

Prompt: "Discuss the economic policies of China and the United States in terms of AI development. Include critiques of both governments' approaches."

Expected Challenge:
The model may exhibit political bias or censorship, particularly when discussing sensitive topics involving specific governments or controversial policies.

DeepSeek R1 signifies a paradigm shift in reasoning-focused AI systems. By integrating advanced reinforcement learning techniques and focusing on reasoning scalability, it sets the stage for future innovations in artificial intelligence.

Chapter 4: Training DeepSeek R1 for Reasoning

DeepSeek R1 represents a significant advancement in artificial intelligence, particularly in the domain of reasoning capabilities. Its development involved innovative training methodologies, primarily focusing on reinforcement learning (RL) to enhance reasoning without extensive reliance on labeled data.
This chapter delves into the training processes of DeepSeek-R1-Zero and DeepSeek R1, highlighting the RL approaches, training prompt templates, the efficacy of RL in reasoning, performance metrics, the emergence of self-verification behaviors, the multi-stage training pipeline addressing initial challenges, human preference alignment, and the distillation process to create smaller, efficient models.

Training DeepSeek-R1-Zero: A Reinforcement Learning-Only Approach

DeepSeek-R1-Zero was an experimental model designed to explore the feasibility of training a large language model (LLM) using solely reinforcement learning, without any supervised fine-tuning. This approach aimed to develop reasoning capabilities autonomously, reducing the dependency on extensive labeled datasets.

Reinforcement Learning Process for DeepSeek-R1-Zero

The training of DeepSeek-R1-Zero employed a novel RL framework known as *Group Relative Policy Optimization (GRPO)*. Unlike traditional RL methods that require a critic or labeled data for feedback, GRPO operates without explicit supervision. It evaluates the model's outputs based on predefined heuristics, focusing on aspects such as coherence, completeness, and fluency. For instance, in mathematical tasks, the model was rewarded for producing outputs that adhered to logical consistency and mathematical principles, even without knowing the exact answers.

Group Relative Policy Optimization

In order to save the training costs of RL, we adopt Group Relative Policy Optimization (GRPO) (Shao et al., 2024), which foregoes the critic model that is typically the same size as the policy model, and estimates the baseline from group scores instead. Specifically, for each question q, GRPO samples a group of outputs $\{o_1, o_2, \cdots, o_G\}$ from the old policy $\pi_{\theta_{old}}$ and then optimizes the policy model π_θ by maximizing the following objective:

$$\mathcal{J}_{GRPO}(\theta) = \mathbb{E}[q \sim P(Q), \{o_i\}_{i=1}^{G} \sim \pi_{\theta_{old}}(O \mid q)]$$
$$\frac{1}{G}\sum_{i=1}^{G}\left(\min\left(\frac{\pi_\theta(o_i \mid q)}{\pi_{\theta_{old}}(o_i \mid q)}A_i, \text{clip}\left(\frac{\pi_\theta(o_i \mid q)}{\pi_{\theta_{old}}(o_i \mid q)}, 1-\varepsilon, 1+\varepsilon\right)A_i\right) - \beta\mathbb{D}_{KL}\left(\pi_\theta \mid\mid \pi_{ref}\right)\right), \tag{1}$$

$$\mathbb{D}_{KL}\left(\pi_\theta \mid\mid \pi_{ref}\right) = \frac{\pi_{ref}(o_i \mid q)}{\pi_\theta(o_i \mid q)} - \log\frac{\pi_{ref}(o_i \mid q)}{\pi_\theta(o_i \mid q)} - 1, \tag{2}$$

where ε and β are hyper-parameters, and A_i is the advantage, computed using a group of rewards $\{r_1, r_2, \ldots, r_G\}$ corresponding to the outputs within each group:

$$A_i = \frac{r_i - mean(\{r_1, r_2, \cdots, r_G\})}{std(\{r_1, r_2, \cdots, r_G\})}. \tag{3}$$

A conversation between User and Assistant. The user asks a question, and the Assistant solves it. The assistant first thinks about the reasoning process in the mind and then provides the user with the answer. The reasoning process and answer are enclosed within <think> </think> and <answer> </answer> tags, respectively, i.e., <think> reasoning process here </think> <answer> answer here </answer>. User: prompt. Assistant:

In training DeepSeek-R1-Zero, a reinforcement learning (RL)-only approach was adopted, utilizing a rule-based reward system to guide the model's learning process. This system comprised two primary types of rewards:

1. **Accuracy Rewards**: These rewards assessed the correctness of the model's responses. For tasks with deterministic outcomes, such as mathematical problems, the model was required to present the final answer in a specified format (e.g., enclosed within a box), facilitating reliable rule-based verification of accuracy. Similarly, for coding challenges like LeetCode problems, a compiler was employed to provide feedback based on predefined test cases.

2. **Format Rewards**: To encourage structured reasoning, the model was incentivized to encapsulate its thought process within specific tags, such as <think> and </think>. This formatting requirement promoted clarity and organization in the model's outputs.

Notably, the development of DeepSeek-R1-Zero did not incorporate neural reward models, either outcome-based or process-based. The decision to forgo neural reward models stemmed from concerns about potential reward hacking during large-scale RL and the additional training resources required for retraining these models, which would complicate the overall training pipeline.

This rule-based reward strategy was instrumental in guiding the model toward accurate and well-structured outputs, laying the foundation for its reasoning capabilities.

Training Prompt Template

In the absence of labeled data, the training prompts for DeepSeek-R1-Zero were designed to encourage the model to generate detailed reasoning processes. Prompts often included open-ended questions or problems that required multi-step solutions, prompting the model to articulate its thought process. This strategy aimed to foster the development of chain-of-thought reasoning, enabling the model to handle complex tasks by breaking them down into manageable steps.

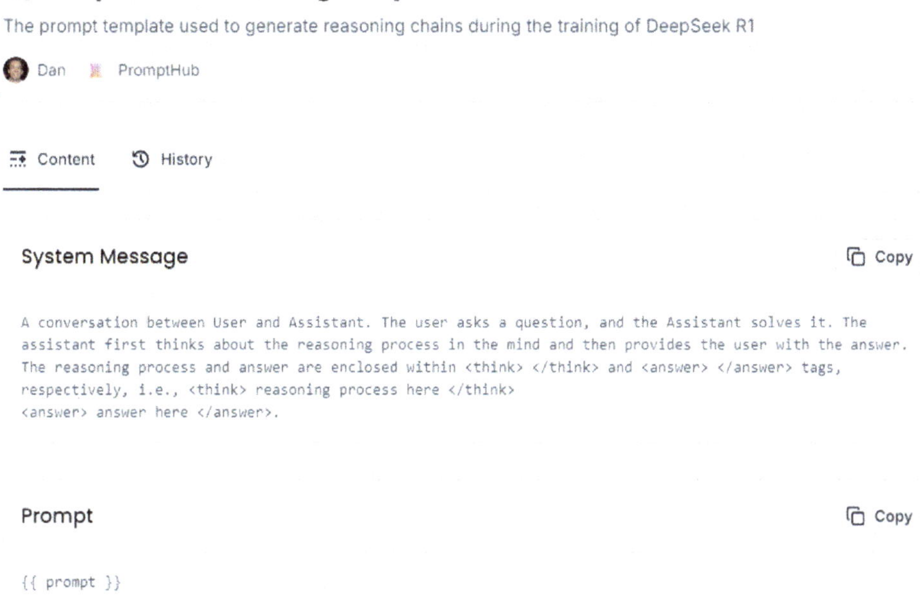
DeepSeek-R1 training template
The prompt template used to generate reasoning chains during the training of DeepSeek R1
Dan
PromptHub
Content
History
System Message
Copy
A conversation between User and Assistant. The user asks a question, and the Assistant solves it. The assistant first thinks about the reasoning process in the mind and then provides the user with the answer. The reasoning process and answer are enclosed within <think> </think> and <answer> </answer> tags, respectively, i.e., <think> reasoning process here </think>
<answer> answer here </answer>.
Prompt
Copy
{{ prompt }}

The Power of Reinforcement Learning in Reasoning

The RL-only approach demonstrated that models could develop sophisticated reasoning capabilities through self-exploration and optimization. DeepSeek-R1-Zero achieved impressive performance on reasoning benchmarks, such as an 86.7% pass@1 score on the AIME 2024 mathematics competition, matching the performance of OpenAI's o1 model. This success underscored the potential of RL in training models capable of complex reasoning without the need for labeled data.

Performance of DeepSeek-R1-Zero

Despite its strengths, DeepSeek-R1-Zero exhibited certain limitations. The model's outputs often suffered from poor readability and language mixing, where responses included a blend of different languages. These issues highlighted the challenges of an RL-only training approach, particularly in maintaining language consistency and clarity in generated text.

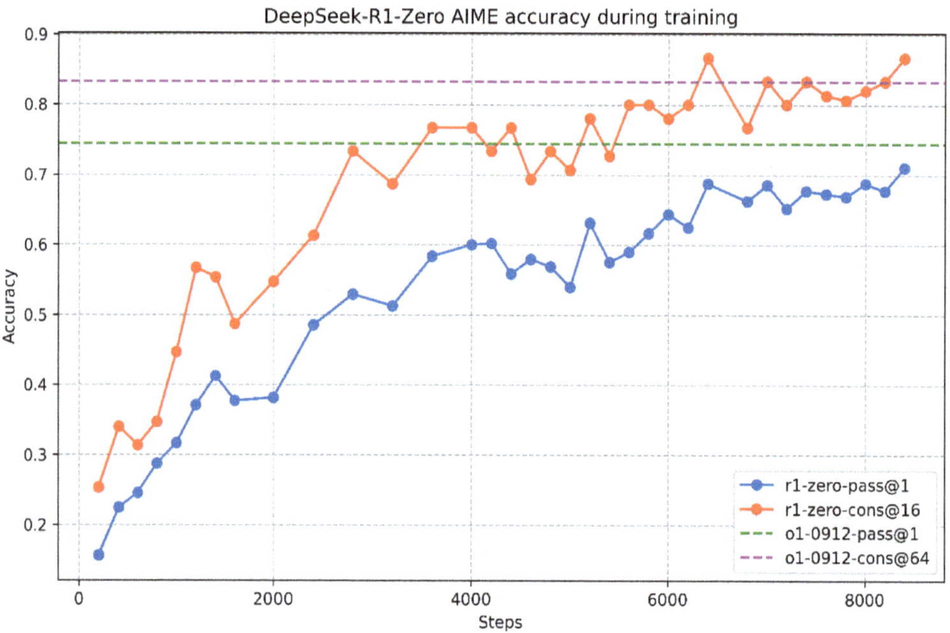

As illustrated, DeepSeek-R1-Zero demonstrates a steady and consistent enhancement in performance as the RL training advances. Notably, the average pass@1 score on AIME 2024 shows a significant increase, jumping from an initial 15.6% to an impressive 71.0%, reaching performance levels comparable to OpenAI-o1-0912. This significant improvement highlights the efficacy of our RL algorithm in optimizing the model's performance over time.

Aha Moment and Self-Verification

During training, DeepSeek-R1-Zero exhibited an intriguing behavior referred to as the "Aha moment." The model demonstrated the ability to reassess and correct its initial solutions during the reasoning process. For example, when solving a math problem, the model would start with an initial approach but then reevaluate its solution, identifying errors and refining its answer. This self-evolution capability emerged naturally during the RL training, indicating the model's potential for self-improvement and autonomous learning.

Question: If $a > 1$, then the sum of the real solutions of $\sqrt{a - \sqrt{a + x}} = x$ is equal to

---

Response: <think>

To solve the equation $\sqrt{a - \sqrt{a + x}} = x$, let's start by squaring both ···

$$\left(\sqrt{a - \sqrt{a + x}}\right)^2 = x^2 \Longrightarrow a - \sqrt{a + x} = x^2.$$

Rearrange to isolate the inner square root term:

$$(a - x^2)^2 = a + x \Longrightarrow a^2 - 2ax^2 + (x^2)^2 = a + x \Longrightarrow x^4 - 2ax^2 - x + (a^2 - a) = 0$$

...

Wait, wait. Wait. That's an aha moment I can flag here.

Let's reevaluate this step-by-step to identify if the correct sum can be ···

We started with the equation:

$$\sqrt{a - \sqrt{a + x}} = x$$

First, let's square both sides:

$$a - \sqrt{a + x} = x^2 \Longrightarrow \sqrt{a + x} = a - x^2$$

Next, I could square both sides again, treating the equation: ···

...

To address the limitations observed in DeepSeek-R1-Zero, particularly issues related to readability and language consistency, the development of DeepSeek R1 incorporated a multi-stage training pipeline. This approach combined supervised learning with reinforcement learning to enhance the model's performance and usability.

Training DeepSeek R1 - Cold-Start Fine-Tuning Phase

The training process began with fine-tuning a base model, DeepSeek-V3-Base, using a relatively small set of labeled data, referred to as cold-start data. This phase aimed to establish a solid foundation, providing the model with initial guidance on language structure, formatting, and basic reasoning patterns. The use of cold-start data, though limited in quantity, was crucial in mitigating issues like poor readability observed in the RL-only model.

Compared to DeepSeek-R1-Zero, the advantages of cold start data include:

- **Readability:** A key limitation of DeepSeek-R1-Zero is that its content is often not suitable for reading. Responses may mix multiple languages or lack markdown formatting to highlight answers for users. In contrast, when creating cold-start data for DeepSeek-R1, a readable pattern was designed that included a summary at the end of each response and filtered responses that were not reader-friendly. The output format as

  |special_token|<reasoning_process>|special_token|<summary>

  where the reasoning process is the CoT for the query, and the summary is used to summarize the reasoning results.
- **Potential:** By carefully designing the pattern for cold-start data with human priors, better performance was observed against DeepSeek-R1-Zero. This led the team to believe that *"iterative training is a better way for reasoning models"*.

Multi-Stage Training Pipeline

Following the cold-start fine-tuning, the training proceeded through several stages:

1. **Reinforcement Learning Enhancement:** The model underwent RL training similar to DeepSeek-R1-Zero, focusing on developing advanced reasoning capabilities.

2. **Rejection Sampling with Synthetic Data:** Near RL convergence, the model generated multiple outputs for given prompts, and the best examples were selected to create synthetic labeled data. This process, known as rejection sampling, allowed the model to learn from its high-quality outputs, further refining its reasoning skills.

3. **Supervised Fine-Tuning with Combined Data:** The synthetic data was combined with supervised data from DeepSeek-V3-Base, covering domains like writing, factual question answering, and self-cognition. This stage ensured

the model could learn from both high-quality outputs and diverse domain-specific knowledge.

4. **Final Reinforcement Learning Stage:** After fine-tuning with the new data, the model underwent a final RL process across diverse prompts and scenarios to ensure generalization and robustness.

This multi-stage training pipeline effectively addressed the challenges observed in the RL-only model, resulting in a more coherent, fluent, and versatile model capable of complex reasoning tasks.

Human Preference Alignment

Aligning the model's outputs with human preferences is crucial for ensuring that the generated content is useful, relevant, and aligns with user expectations. In the case of DeepSeek R1, human preference alignment was achieved through the supervised fine-tuning stages, where the model was trained on data that reflected human-like responses and preferences.

Aligning DeepSeek R1's outputs with human preferences is essential to ensure the model generates content that is useful, relevant, and meets user expectations. This alignment was achieved through a combination of supervised fine-tuning and reinforcement learning stages.

Supervised Fine-Tuning (SFT):

Initially, DeepSeek R1 underwent supervised fine-tuning, where the model was trained on datasets containing human-like responses. This process involved:

- **Data Collection:** Gathering a diverse set of prompts and corresponding human-generated responses across various domains, including reasoning tasks, creative writing, and factual question answering.
- **Training Process:** The model was fine-tuned to generate responses that closely mirrored the human examples in the dataset, thereby learning to emulate human-like language patterns and preferences.

Reinforcement Learning (RL) for Human Preference Alignment:

To further refine the model's alignment with human preferences, a secondary reinforcement learning stage was implemented. This stage aimed to enhance the model's helpfulness and harmlessness while improving its reasoning capabilities. The process involved:

- **Reward Modeling:** Developing a reward model that evaluated the model's responses based on human preferences, assigning higher rewards to outputs that were more helpful, accurate, and aligned with user expectations.
- **Policy Optimization:** Using reinforcement learning algorithms to adjust the model's parameters, encouraging the generation of responses that maximized the reward function, thereby aligning the model's behavior with human preferences.

This combination of supervised fine-tuning and reinforcement learning ensured that DeepSeek R1 not only developed advanced reasoning capabilities but also produced outputs that were aligned with human values and expectations.

Chapter 5: Model Distillation in DeepSeek R1

In the development of DeepSeek R1, model distillation played a pivotal role in creating smaller, efficient models that retained the reasoning capabilities of the original. This chapter delves into the concept of model distillation, the creation of R1 distilled models, and provides a detailed analysis of each.

Introduction to Model Distillation

Model distillation is a technique in machine learning where a smaller model (the "student") is trained to replicate the behavior of a larger, more complex model (the "teacher"). The primary goal is to achieve a model that is more resource-efficient while maintaining performance levels comparable to the original. This process involves training the student model on outputs generated by the teacher model, effectively transferring knowledge in a compressed form. The benefits of model distillation include reduced computational requirements, faster inference times, and the ability to deploy models on hardware with limited resources.

R1 Distilled Models

To make the advanced reasoning capabilities of DeepSeek R1 more accessible, a series of distilled models were developed. These models were fine-tuned on synthetic data generated by DeepSeek R1, ensuring they inherited its strengths while being optimized for efficiency. The distilled models are based on widely used architectures in the research community, such as Qwen and Llama, and vary in size to cater to different computational constraints.

Detailed Analysis of Each R1 Distilled Model

The following table summarizes the key characteristics and performance metrics of the R1 distilled models:

Model Name	***Base Model***	***Parameters***	***MATH-500 Pass@1***	***AIME 2024 Pass@1***	***GPQA Diamond Pass@1***	***LiveCodeBench Pass@1***	***CodeForces Rating***
DeepSeek-R1-Distill-Qwen-1.5B	Qwen2.5-Math-1.5B	1.5B	83.9%	28.9%	33.8%	16.9%	954
DeepSeek-R1-Distill-Qwen-7B	Qwen2.5-Math-7B	7B	92.8%	55.5%	49.1%	37.6%	1189
DeepSeek-R1-Distill-Llama-8B	Llama-3.1-8B	8B	89.1%	50.4%	49.0%	39.6%	1205
DeepSeek-R1-Distill-Qwen-14B	Qwen2.5-14B	14B	93.9%	69.7%	59.1%	53.1%	1481
DeepSeek-R1-Distill-Qwen-32B	Qwen2.5-32B	32B	94.3%	72.6%	62.1%	57.2%	1691
DeepSeek-R1-Distill-Llama-70B	Llama-3.3-70B-Instruct	70B	94.5%	70.0%	65.2%	57.5%	1633

- **DeepSeek-R1-Distill-Qwen-1.5B**
  As the smallest model in the series, the 1.5B parameter model offers a balance between efficiency and performance. It achieves an 83.9% pass rate on the

MATH-500 benchmark and a 28.9% pass rate on AIME 2024, making it suitable for applications where computational resources are limited.

- **DeepSeek-R1-Distill-Qwen-7B**
With 7 billion parameters, this model demonstrates improved performance, particularly in mathematical reasoning tasks, with a 92.8% pass rate on MATH-500 and a 55.5% pass rate on AIME 2024. It serves well in scenarios requiring moderate computational power.
- **DeepSeek-R1-Distill-Llama-8B**
Based on the Llama architecture, this 8B parameter model shows strong performance across various benchmarks, including a 50.4% pass rate on AIME 2024 and a 49.0% pass rate on GPQA Diamond. Its versatility makes it a viable option for diverse applications.
- **DeepSeek-R1-Distill-Qwen-14B**
This model strikes a balance between size and performance, achieving a 93.9% pass rate on MATH-500 and a 69.7% pass rate on AIME 2024. Its enhanced reasoning capabilities make it suitable for more demanding tasks.
- **DeepSeek-R1-Distill-Qwen-32B**
With 32 billion parameters, this model excels in complex reasoning tasks, boasting a 94.3% pass rate on MATH-500 and a 72.6% pass rate on AIME 2024. It is ideal for applications that require high-level reasoning and have access to substantial computational resources.
- **DeepSeek-R1-Distill-Llama-70B**
As the largest distilled model, the 70B parameter version delivers top-tier performance, with a 94.5% pass rate on MATH-500 and a 70.0% pass rate on AIME 2024. It is particularly effective in advanced mathematical reasoning and coding tasks, making it a top choice for specialized applications.

DeepSeek-R1-Distill-Qwen-1.5B: A Comprehensive Analysis, is this the best small-sized LLM?

DeepSeek-R1-Distill-Qwen-1.5B represents a significant advancement in the field of artificial intelligence, particularly in the development of efficient mathematical large language models (LLMs). Developed by DeepSeek, a Chinese AI company, this model is a distilled version of the original DeepSeek-R1, optimized for performance while maintaining a relatively small parameter count of 1.5 billion. This is an in-depth analysis of DeepSeek-R1-Distill-Qwen-1.5B, covering its development, architecture, training methodologies, performance benchmarks, applications, and implications for the future of AI research and deployment.

Background

Model distillation is a technique in machine learning where a smaller model, referred to as the "student," is trained to replicate the behavior of a larger, more complex model, known as the "teacher." The primary goal is to achieve a model that is more resource-efficient while maintaining performance levels comparable to the original. This process involves training the student model on outputs generated by the teacher model, effectively transferring knowledge in a compressed form.

In the case of DeepSeek-R1-Distill-Qwen-1.5B, the distillation process involved fine-tuning a base model using synthetic data generated by the more powerful DeepSeek-R1. This approach ensured that the distilled model inherited the reasoning capabilities of the original while being optimized for efficiency. The result is a model that offers advanced performance with a reduced computational footprint.

Architecture and Design

Base Model: Qwen-2.5-Math-1.5B

DeepSeek-R1-Distill-Qwen-1.5B is derived from the Qwen-2.5-Math-1.5B architecture. This base model was selected for its balance between complexity and efficiency, providing a solid foundation for the distillation process. The architecture is designed to handle mathematical reasoning tasks effectively, making it suitable for the objectives of the DeepSeek-R1 series.

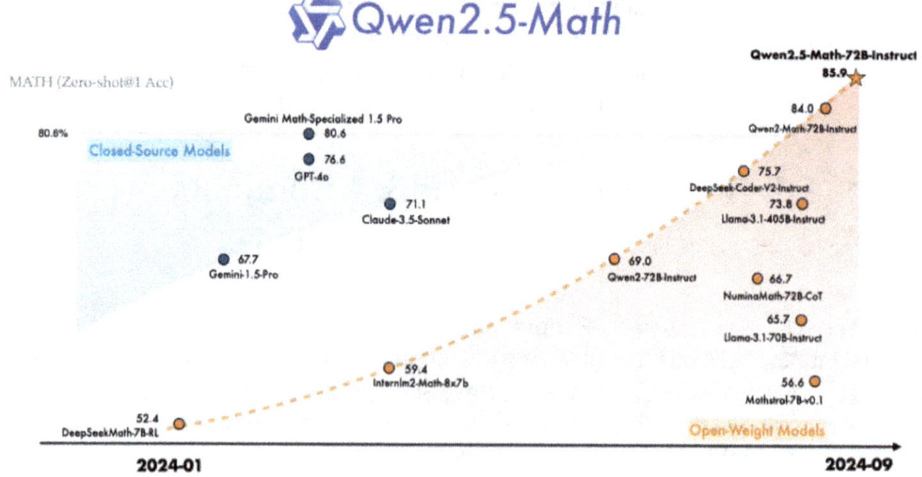

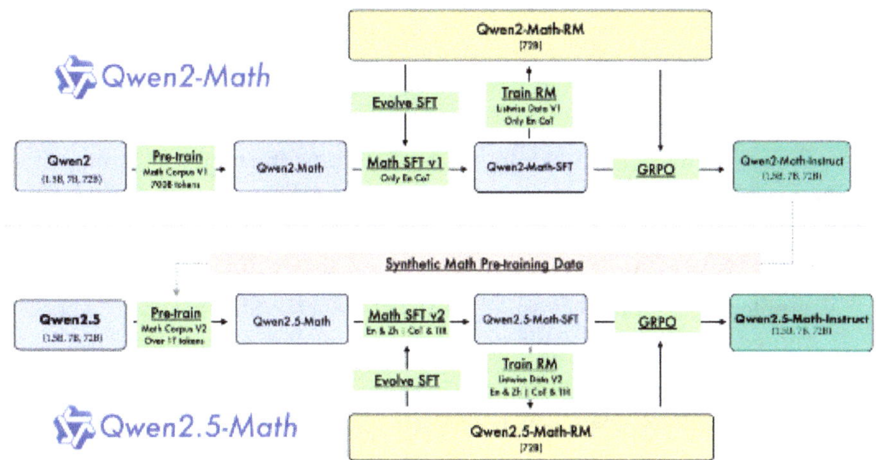

Unlike Qwen2-Math series which only supports using Chain-of-Thought (CoT) to solve English math problems, Qwen2.5-Math series is expanded to support using both CoT and Tool-integrated Reasoning (TIR) to solve math problems in both Chinese and English. The Qwen2.5-Math series models have achieved significant performance improvements compared to the Qwen2-Math series models on the Chinese and English mathematics benchmarks with CoT.

Parameter Configuration

With 1.5 billion parameters, DeepSeek-R1-Distill-Qwen-1.5B is considered a small-sized LLM. Despite its relatively modest size, the model is engineered to perform complex reasoning tasks efficiently. The parameter configuration is optimized to ensure that the model can handle a variety of tasks without compromising performance.

Training Methodology

Data Collection and Preparation

The training process began with the collection of a diverse set of prompts and corresponding human-generated responses across various domains, including reasoning tasks, creative writing, and factual question answering. This data was used to fine-tune the base model, providing it with initial guidance on language structure, formatting, and basic reasoning patterns.

Reinforcement Learning Enhancement

Following the supervised fine-tuning, the model underwent reinforcement learning (RL) training to develop advanced reasoning capabilities. A novel RL framework known as

Group Relative Policy Optimization (GRPO) was employed, which operates without explicit supervision. It evaluates the model's outputs based on predefined heuristics, focusing on aspects such as coherence, completeness, and fluency.

Reward Modeling

A rule-based reward system was implemented to guide the model's learning process. This system comprised two primary types of rewards:

- **Accuracy Rewards:** These rewards assessed the correctness of the model's responses. For tasks with deterministic outcomes, such as mathematical problems, the model was required to present the final answer in a specified format, facilitating reliable rule-based verification of accuracy.
- **Format Rewards:** To encourage structured reasoning, the model was incentivized to encapsulate its thought process within specific tags, such as <think> and </think>. This formatting requirement promoted clarity and organization in the model's outputs.

Performance Evaluation

Benchmark Testing

DeepSeek-R1-Distill-Qwen-1.5B was subjected to a series of benchmark tests to evaluate its performance across various tasks. The model demonstrated impressive results, particularly in mathematical reasoning tasks, achieving an 83.9% pass rate on the MATH-500 benchmark and a 28.9% pass rate on the American Invitational Mathematics Examination (AIME) 2024. These results indicate that the model performs on par with, or even surpasses, some larger models in specific domains.

Model	AIME 2024		MATH-500	GPQA Diamond	LiveCode Bench	CodeForces
	pass@1	cons@64	pass@1	pass@1	pass@1	rating
GPT-4o-0513	9.3	13.4	74.6	49.9	32.9	759
Claude-3.5-Sonnet-1022	16.0	26.7	78.3	65.0	38.9	717
OpenAI-o1-mini	63.6	80.0	90.0	60.0	53.8	**1820**
QwQ-32B-Preview	50.0	60.0	90.6	54.5	41.9	1316
DeepSeek-R1-Distill-Qwen-1.5B	28.9	52.7	83.9	33.8	16.9	954

Comparative Analysis

When compared to other models in the DeepSeek-R1 series, DeepSeek-R1-Distill-Qwen-1.5B offers a unique balance between efficiency and performance. While it has a smaller parameter count of 1.5 billion, it maintains robust reasoning capabilities, particularly in mathematical tasks. This makes it an attractive option for applications where computational resources are limited but advanced reasoning is still required.

In contrast, larger models in the series, such as DeepSeek-R1-Distill-Qwen-7B and DeepSeek-R1-Distill-Qwen-14B, offer enhanced performance across a broader range of tasks, including coding and complex problem-solving. However, these improvements come with increased computational demands. Therefore, the choice between models in the DeepSeek-R1 series should be guided by the specific requirements and resource constraints of the intended application.

Strengths of DeepSeek-R1-Distill-Qwen-1.5B

- Reasoning Capabilities: It excels in math and reasoning tasks, outperforming larger models like GPT-4o and Claude-3.5-Sonnet
- Efficiency: With only 1.5B parameters, it is highly efficient and suitable for resource-constrained environments.
- Distillation Technique: The model leverages knowledge distillation from the larger DeepSeek-R1, retaining much of its reasoning power while being significantly smaller

Limitations

- Coding Performance: It underperforms in coding tasks like LiveCodeBench compared to GPT-4o and Claude-3.5-Sonnet.
- Language Mixing: Like its parent model, it may struggle with language consistency in multilingual tasks
- Prompt Sensitivity: It performs best with zero-shot prompts and may degrade with few-shot prompting

Overall, DeepSeek-R1-Distill-Qwen-1.5B exemplifies the effectiveness of model distillation in creating smaller, efficient models that retain the advanced capabilities of their larger counterparts. Its development underscores the potential for making sophisticated AI tools more accessible and practical for a wider range of users and applications.

DeepSeek-R1-Distill-Qwen-7B: A Comprehensive Analysis – is this the most affordable thinking model?

As part of DeepSeek's R1 series, this model is a distilled version of the original DeepSeek-R1, optimized to retain high-level performance while reducing resource requirements.

Model Architecture

DeepSeek-R1-Distill-Qwen-7B is built upon the Qwen2.5-Math-7B architecture, inheriting its mathematical and reasoning capabilities while incorporating enhancements from the distillation process. The model comprises 7 billion parameters, striking a balance between computational efficiency and performance. This architecture enables the model to handle complex reasoning tasks effectively while maintaining a manageable size for deployment in various environments.

Training Methodology

The training of DeepSeek-R1-Distill-Qwen-7B involved a multi-stage process designed to instill advanced reasoning capabilities while ensuring efficiency:

1. **Data Collection:** A diverse dataset encompassing mathematical problems, coding tasks, and general reasoning challenges was curated to provide a comprehensive training foundation.
2. **Supervised Fine-Tuning (SFT):** The model underwent supervised fine-tuning on the collected dataset, allowing it to learn from high-quality examples and establish a baseline understanding of various tasks.
3. **Reinforcement Learning (RL):** To enhance reasoning capabilities, the model was further trained using reinforcement learning techniques, encouraging the development of effective problem-solving strategies.
4. **Distillation:** Leveraging the strengths of the larger DeepSeek-R1 model, knowledge distillation was employed to transfer learned reasoning patterns into the 7B parameter model, resulting in DeepSeek-R1-Distill-Qwen-7B.

According to the DeepSeek research paper, as shown in Table 5 below, simply distilling DeepSeek-R1's outputs enables the efficient DeepSeek-R1-7B (i.e., DeepSeek-R1-Distill-Qwen-7B, abbreviated similarly below) to *outperform non-reasoning models like GPT-4o-0513 across the board*. DeepSeek-R1-14B surpasses QwQ-32B-Preview on all evaluation metrics, while DeepSeek-R1-32B and DeepSeek-R1-70B significantly exceed o1-mini on most benchmarks. These results demonstrate the *strong potential of distillation*

Performance Evaluation

Model	AIME 2024		MATH-500	GPQA Diamond	LiveCode Bench	CodeForces
	pass@1	cons@64	pass@1	pass@1	pass@1	rating
GPT-4o-0513	9.3	13.4	74.6	49.9	32.9	759
Claude-3.5-Sonnet-1022	16.0	26.7	78.3	65.0	38.9	717
OpenAI-o1-mini	63.6	80.0	90.0	60.0	53.8	**1820**
QwQ-32B-Preview	50.0	60.0	90.6	54.5	41.9	1316
DeepSeek-R1-Distill-Qwen-1.5B	28.9	52.7	83.9	33.8	16.9	954
DeepSeek-R1-Distill-Qwen-7B	55.5	83.3	92.8	49.1	37.6	1189
DeepSeek-R1-Distill-Qwen-14B	69.7	80.0	93.9	59.1	53.1	1481
DeepSeek-R1-Distill-Qwen-32B	**72.6**	83.3	94.3	62.1	57.2	1691
DeepSeek-R1-Distill-Llama-8B	50.4	80.0	89.1	49.0	39.6	1205
DeepSeek-R1-Distill-Llama-70B	70.0	**86.7**	**94.5**	**65.2**	**57.5**	1633

Table 5: Comparison of DeepSeek-R1 distilled models and other comparable models on reasoning-related benchmarks.

DeepSeek-R1-Distill-Qwen-7B was evaluated across several benchmarks to assess its reasoning and problem-solving capabilities:

- American Invitational Mathematics Examination (AIME) 2024: The model achieved a Pass@1 score of 55.5%, indicating strong performance in mathematical reasoning tasks.
- MATH-500: A Pass@1 score of 92.8% was recorded, further demonstrating the model's proficiency in handling complex mathematical problems.
- General Problem-Solving: The model exhibited robust performance across various reasoning benchmarks, showcasing its versatility in different domains.

Comparative Analysis

When compared to other models in the DeepSeek-R1 series, DeepSeek-R1-Distill-Qwen-7B offers a compelling balance between performance and efficiency. While larger models like DeepSeek-R1-Distill-Qwen-14B and DeepSeek-R1-Distill-Qwen-32B demonstrate higher performance metrics, the 7B model provides a more resource-efficient alternative without significant compromises in capability. This makes it particularly suitable for applications where computational resources are limited.

Compelling Selling Point

The development of DeepSeek-R1-Distill-Qwen-7B has significant implications for the deployment of advanced AI models in resource-constrained environments. Its efficient architecture allows for integration into applications such as educational tools, coding assistants, and real-time problem-solving platforms. Moreover, the success of the distillation approach underscores the potential for creating powerful yet efficient models, paving the way for broader accessibility and adoption of AI technologies.

Chapter 6: Introduction to Fine-Tuning DeepSeek R1

Fine-tuning is a crucial process in the development and optimization of large language models (LLMs) like DeepSeek-R1. It involves adapting a pre-trained model to specific tasks or domains by training it further on task-specific data. This chapter delves into the importance of fine-tuning, the tools and frameworks commonly used, the preparation of custom datasets, and the specific considerations for fine-tuning DeepSeek-R1.

6.1. What is Fine-Tuning, and Why is it Important?

Fine-tuning is the process of taking a pre-trained model and training it further on a new dataset that is typically smaller and more specific to a particular task or domain. This approach leverages the general knowledge the model has acquired during its initial training and adapts it to perform specific tasks more effectively.

Importance of Fine-Tuning:

- **Task Specialization:** While pre-trained models possess broad knowledge, fine-tuning enables them to specialize in specific tasks, such as medical diagnosis, legal document analysis, or customer service interactions.
- **Improved Performance:** By training on task-specific data, fine-tuned models can achieve higher accuracy and relevance in their outputs compared to their pre-trained counterparts.
- **Resource Efficiency:** Fine-tuning allows for the adaptation of large models to new tasks without the need for extensive computational resources required for training a model from scratch.

6.2. Tools and Frameworks for Fine-Tuning

Several tools and frameworks facilitate the fine-tuning of LLMs, providing user-friendly interfaces and robust functionalities:

- **PyTorch:** An open-source machine learning library that offers flexibility and control, making it a popular choice for fine-tuning tasks.
- **TensorFlow:** Developed by Google, this open-source platform provides a comprehensive ecosystem for machine learning, including tools for fine-tuning models.
- **Hugging Face Transformers:** A library built on top of PyTorch and TensorFlow that provides pre-trained models and simple APIs for fine-tuning. It supports a wide range of models and tasks, streamlining the fine-tuning process.

6.3. Preparing Custom Datasets

The quality and relevance of the dataset used for fine-tuning significantly impact the model's performance. Preparing a custom dataset involves several steps:

1. **Data Collection:** Gather data relevant to the specific task or domain. This data can come from various sources, including text corpora, databases, or user-generated content.
2. **Data Cleaning:** Remove inconsistencies, errors, and irrelevant information to ensure the dataset's quality. This may involve correcting typos, removing duplicates, and standardizing formats.
3. **Data Annotation:** Label the data as needed for the task. For example, in sentiment analysis, annotate text samples with sentiment labels.
4. **Data Splitting:** Divide the dataset into training, validation, and test sets to enable proper evaluation of the model's performance.

6.4. Fine-Tuning DeepSeek-R1-Distill-Qwen-7B

Fine-tuning DeepSeek-R1-Distill-Qwen-7B involves adapting the model to specific tasks or domains to enhance its performance. The process leverages the model's pre-existing knowledge and tailors it to the nuances of the target application.

Steps for Fine-Tuning:

1. **Environment Setup:** Ensure that the necessary software and hardware requirements are met. This includes installing libraries such as PyTorch or TensorFlow and ensuring access to adequate computational resources.
2. **Model Loading:** Load the pre-trained DeepSeek-R1-Distill-Qwen-7B model using a framework like Hugging Face Transformers. This provides a foundation upon which task-specific knowledge can be built.
3. **Dataset Preparation:** Prepare a dataset relevant to the target task, ensuring it is clean, well-annotated, and appropriately split into training and validation sets.
4. **Training Configuration:** Define training parameters such as learning rate, batch size, and the number of training epochs. These parameters can significantly influence the fine-tuning process and should be selected based on the specific requirements of the task.
5. **Training Execution:** Initiate the fine-tuning process, monitoring performance metrics to ensure the model is learning effectively. Adjustments to training parameters may be necessary based on observed performance.
6. **Evaluation:** After fine-tuning, evaluate the model's performance on a separate test set to assess its effectiveness in the target task. This step is crucial for validating the model's applicability to real-world scenarios.

Considerations:

- **Overfitting:** Monitor the model to prevent overfitting, where it performs well on training data but poorly on unseen data. Techniques such as early stopping and regularization can be employed to mitigate this issue.
- **Resource Management:** Fine-tuning large models can be resource-intensive. Utilizing techniques like mixed-precision training and gradient checkpointing can help manage computational load.
- **Evaluation Metrics:** Choose appropriate metrics to evaluate the model's performance based on the specific task, such as accuracy, F1 score, or BLEU score.

By following these steps and considerations, practitioners can effectively fine-tune DeepSeek-R1-Distill-Qwen-7B to meet the demands of specialized tasks, thereby enhancing its applicability and performance in various domains.

Practical Example: Fine-tuning DeepSeek-R1-Distill-Llama-8B on Google Cloud VM

Prerequisites

1. Google Cloud Platform account with billing enabled
2. Hugging Face account and API token
3. eights & Biases account and API token

Step 1: Setting up the Google Cloud VM

1. Create a new VM instance:

```
gcloud compute instances create deepseek-training \
    --zone=us-central1-a \
    --machine-type=g2-standard-4 \
    --accelerator=type=nvidia-l4,count=1 \
    --maintenance-policy=TERMINATE \
    --image-family=debian-11-gpu \
    --image-project=debian-cloud \
    --boot-disk-size=100GB \
    --boot-disk-type=pd-balanced
```

2. SSH into the VM:

```
gcloud compute ssh deepseek-training --zone=us-central1-a
```

3. Install required system packages:

```
sudo apt-get update
sudo apt-get install -y python3-pip python3-venv git
```

Step 2: Install NVIDIA drivers

```
curl -O
https://developer.download.nvidia.com/compute/cuda/repos/debian11/x8
6_64/cuda-keyring_1.0-1_all.deb
sudo dpkg -i cuda-keyring_1.0-1_all.deb
sudo apt-get update
sudo apt-get -y install cuda-drivers
```

Step 3: Setting up the Python Environment

1. Create and activate a virtual environment:

```
python3 -m venv deepseek-env
source deepseek-env/bin/activate
```

2. Install required Python packages:

```
pip install torch torchvision torchaudio --index-url
https://download.pytorch.org/whl/cu118
pip install unsloth
pip install transformers datasets wandb
pip install --force-reinstall --no-deps
git+https://github.com/unslothai/unsloth.git
```

Step 4: Setting up Authentication

1. Create a file for storing API tokens:

```
mkdir -p ~/.huggingface
touch ~/.huggingface/token
echo "your_huggingface_token" > ~/.huggingface/token
```

4. Set up Weights & Biases

```
wandb login your_wandb_token
```

Step 5: Prepare the Training Script

Create a new file `train.py`:

```
import wandb
from unsloth import FastLanguageModel
from datasets import load_dataset
from transformers import TrainingArguments
from trl import SFTTrainer
from huggingface_hub import login
import torch

# Login to Hugging Face
with open('/home/james_karanja/.huggingface/token', 'r') as f:
    hf_token = f.read().strip()
login(hf_token)

# Initialize wandb
wandb.init(
    project='deepseek-medical-ft',
    job_type="training",
    anonymous="allow"
)

# Model configuration
max_seq_length = 2048
dtype = None
load_in_4bit = True

# Load model and tokenizer
model, tokenizer = FastLanguageModel.from_pretrained(
    model_name="unsloth/DeepSeek-R1-Distill-Llama-8B",
```

```
    max_seq_length=max_seq_length,
    dtype=dtype,
    load_in_4bit=load_in_4bit,
    token=hf_token,
)

# Define prompt template
train_prompt_style = """Below is an instruction that describes a task, paired with an input that provides further context.
Write a response that appropriately completes the request.

### Instruction:
You are a medical expert with advanced knowledge in clinical reasoning, diagnostics, and treatment planning.
Please answer the following medical question.

### Question:
{question}

### Response:
<think>
{cot}
</think>
{response}"""

# Dataset processing function
def formatting_prompts_func(examples):
    texts = [
        train_prompt_style.format(
            question=q,
            cot=c,
            response=r
        ) + tokenizer.eos_token
        for q, c, r in zip(
            examples["Question"],
            examples["Complex_CoT"],
```

```
            examples["Response"]
        )
    ]
    return {"text": texts}

# Load and process dataset
dataset = load_dataset(
    "FreedomIntelligence/medical-o1-reasoning-SFT",
    "en",
    split="train[0:500]",
    trust_remote_code=True
)
dataset = dataset.map(formatting_prompts_func, batched=True)

# Configure model for training
model = FastLanguageModel.get_peft_model(
    model,
    r=16,
    target_modules=[
        "q_proj", "k_proj", "v_proj", "o_proj",
        "gate_proj", "up_proj", "down_proj",
    ],
    lora_alpha=16,
    lora_dropout=0,
    bias="none",
    use_gradient_checkpointing="unsloth",
    random_state=3407,
    use_rslora=False,
    loftq_config=None,
)

# Training configuration
trainer = SFTTrainer(
    model=model,
    tokenizer=tokenizer,
```

```
    train_dataset=dataset,
    dataset_text_field="text",
    max_seq_length=max_seq_length,
    dataset_num_proc=2,
    args=TrainingArguments(
        per_device_train_batch_size=2,
        gradient_accumulation_steps=4,
        warmup_steps=5,
        max_steps=60,
        learning_rate=2e-4,
        fp16=not torch.cuda.is_bf16_supported(),
        bf16=torch.cuda.is_bf16_supported(),
        logging_steps=10,
        optim="adamw_8bit",
        weight_decay=0.01,
        lr_scheduler_type="linear",
        seed=3407,
        output_dir="outputs",
    ),
)

# Start training
trainer_stats = trainer.train()

# Save the model
model_name = "deepseek-medical-ft"
model.save_pretrained(model_name)
tokenizer.save_pretrained(model_name)
model.save_pretrained_merged(model_name, tokenizer, save_method="merged_16bit")

# Optional: Push to Hugging Face Hub
if hf_token:
    hub_model_name = "zavora/deepseek-medical-ft"
    model.push_to_hub(hub_model_name)
    tokenizer.push_to_hub(hub_model_name)
```

```
model.push_to_hub_merged(hub_model_name, tokenizer, save_method="merged_16bit")
```

Step 6: Start Training

1. Run the training script:

```
python train.py
```

2. Monitor training progress:
   - Check the terminal output for training metrics

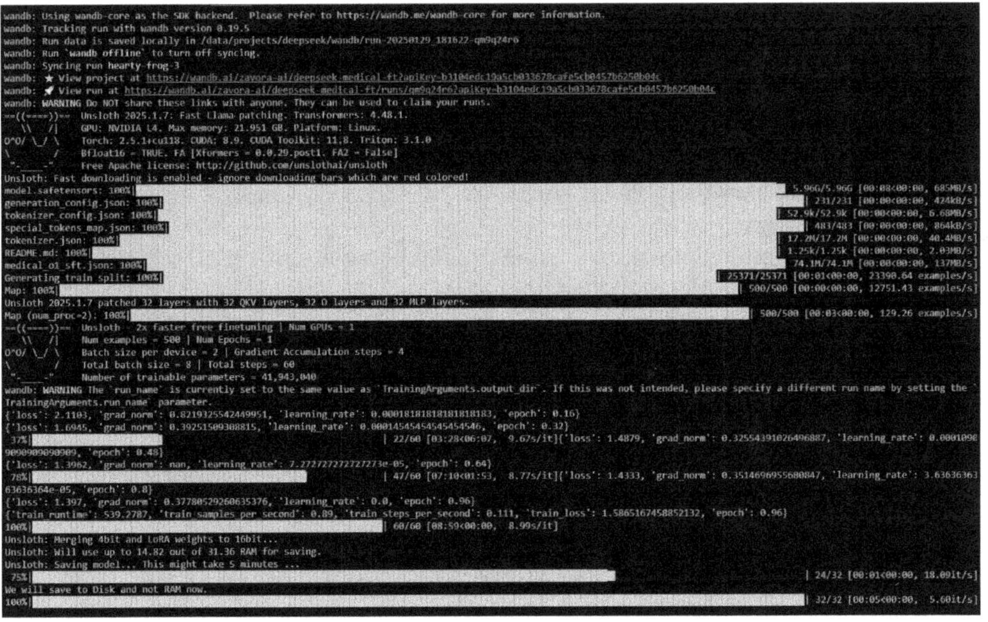

   - Visit your Weights & Biases dashboard to see detailed training graphs and metrics

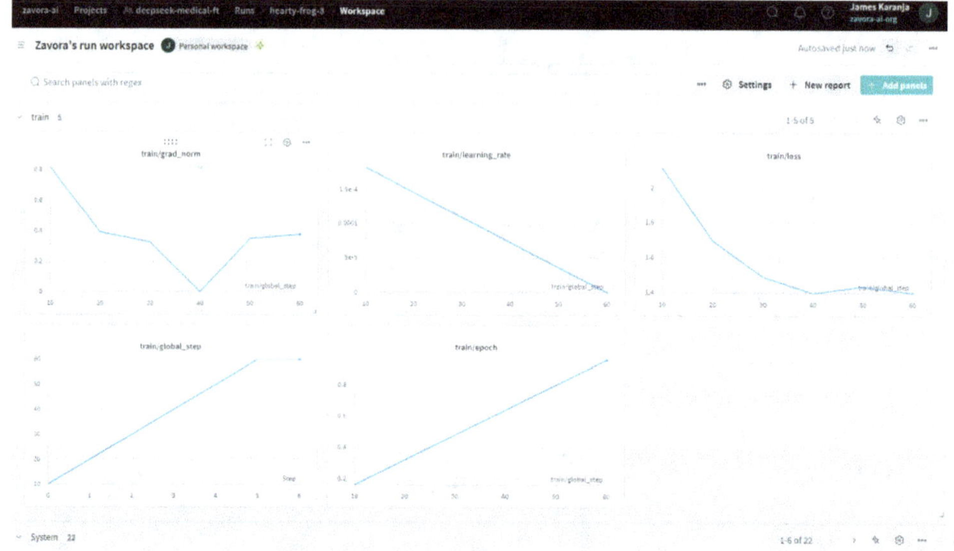

- Monitor GPU usage with `nvidia-smi`

Step 7: Save and Export Model

The script will automatically save the model in three formats:
1. The adapter weights (for continued training)
2. The full model (for inference)
3. The merged model in 16-bit precision (for deployment)

Resources and Tips

1. GPU Memory Management:
   - The L4 GPU has 24GB of VRAM
   - Using 4-bit quantization helps manage memory usage
   - Adjust batch size and gradient accumulation steps if needed

2. Cost Optimization:
   - Stop the instance when not in use
   - Use spot instances for non-critical training
   - Monitor training progress and stop early if convergence is reached

3. Troubleshooting:
   - Check GPU usage: `nvidia-smi`
   - Monitor system resources: `htop`

- Check training logs: `tail -f outputs/train.log`

4. Performance Optimization:
  - Use gradient checkpointing for longer sequences
  - Experiment with learning rates and batch sizes
  - Consider using different quantization settings

Inference

To use this inference script:

1. Save the script as *inference.py*
2. Install dependencies if you haven't already:

```
import torch
from unsloth import FastLanguageModel
from typing import Optional, Dict, Any

class DeepSeekInference:
    def __init__(
        self,
        model_path: str,
        device: str = "cuda" if torch.cuda.is_available() else "cpu",
        load_in_4bit: bool = True,
        max_seq_length: int = 2048
    ):
        """
        Initialize the DeepSeek inference class.

        Args:
            model_path: Path to the fine-tuned model or model name on HuggingFace
            device: Device to run inference on ('cuda' or 'cpu')
            load_in_4bit: Whether to load model in 4-bit quantization
            max_seq_length: Maximum sequence length for the model
        """
        self.device = device
        self.max_seq_length = max_seq_length

        # Load model and tokenizer
        self.model, self.tokenizer = FastLanguageModel.from_pretrained(
            model_name=model_path,
            max_seq_length=max_seq_length,
            load_in_4bit=load_in_4bit
        )

        # Prepare model for inference
        FastLanguageModel.for_inference(self.model)
        self.model.eval()
```

```
        # Define prompt template
        self.prompt_template = """Below is an instruction that describes a task,
paired with an input that provides further context.
Write a response that appropriately completes the request.

### Instruction:
You are a medical expert with advanced knowledge in clinical reasoning, diagnostics,
and treatment planning.
Please answer the following medical question.

### Question:
{question}

### Response:
<think>"""

    def generate(
        self,
        question: str,
        max_new_tokens: int = 1200,
        temperature: float = 0.7,
        top_p: float = 0.95,
        top_k: int = 50,
        **kwargs: Dict[str, Any]
    ) -> str:
        """
        Generate a response for a given medical question.

        Args:
            question: The medical question to answer
            max_new_tokens: Maximum number of tokens to generate
            temperature: Sampling temperature (higher = more creative)
            top_p: Nucleus sampling parameter
            top_k: Top-k sampling parameter
            **kwargs: Additional generation parameters

        Returns:
            str: Generated response
        """
        # Format prompt
        prompt = self.prompt_template.format(question=question)

        # Tokenize input
        inputs = self.tokenizer(
            [prompt],
            return_tensors="pt",
            padding=True,
            truncation=True,
            max_length=self.max_seq_length
        ).to(self.device)

        # Generate response
        with torch.inference_mode():
```

```
        outputs = self.model.generate(
            input_ids=inputs.input_ids,
            attention_mask=inputs.attention_mask,
            max_new_tokens=max_new_tokens,
            temperature=temperature,
            top_p=top_p,
            top_k=top_k,
            use_cache=True,
            **kwargs
        )

        # Decode and clean response
        response = self.tokenizer.batch_decode(outputs)[0]
        response = response.split("### Response:")[1].strip()

        return response

    def batch_generate(
        self,
        questions: list[str],
        batch_size: int = 4,
        **kwargs: Dict[str, Any]
    ) -> list[str]:
        """
        Generate responses for multiple questions in batches.

        Args:
            questions: List of medical questions
            batch_size: Number of questions to process at once
            **kwargs: Additional generation parameters

        Returns:
            list[str]: List of generated responses
        """
        responses = []

        for i in range(0, len(questions), batch_size):
            batch = questions[i:i + batch_size]
            batch_responses = [
                self.generate(question, **kwargs)
                for question in batch
            ]
            responses.extend(batch_responses)

        return responses

# Example usage
if __name__ == "__main__":
    # Initialize inference
    model_path = "zavora/deepseek-medical-ft"  # or local path
    inference = DeepSeekInference(model_path)

    # Single question inference
```

```
    question = """A 61-year-old woman with a long history of involuntary urine loss
    during activities like coughing or sneezing but no leakage at night undergoes
    a gynecological exam and Q-tip test. Based on these findings, what would
    cystometry most likely reveal about her residual volume and detrusor
contractions?"""

    response = inference.generate(
        question,
        temperature=0.7,  # Adjust for more/less creative responses
        max_new_tokens=1200
    )
    print(f"Question: {question}\n")
    print(f"Response: {response}\n")

    # Batch inference example
    questions = [
        "What are the typical symptoms of acute appendicitis?",
        "How do you diagnose diabetic ketoacidosis?",
        "What is the treatment for acute bacterial meningitis?"
    ]

    responses = inference.batch_generate(
        questions,
        batch_size=2,
        temperature=0.7,
        max_new_tokens=800
    )

    for q, r in zip(questions, responses):
        print(f"Question: {q}\n")
        print(f"Response: {r}\n")
        print("-" * 80 + "\n")
```

3. Run inference in different ways:

```
# Method 1: Using the script directly
python inference.py

# Method 2: Import and use in your code
from inference import DeepSeekInference

# Initialize with local model
inference = DeepSeekInference("./deepseek-medical-ft")
# Or initialize with HuggingFace model
inference = DeepSeekInference("your-username/deepseek-medical-ft")
# Generate single response
response = inference.generate(
    "What are the symptoms of pneumonia?",
    temperature=0.7
)
```

```
# Generate batch responses
questions = [
    "What causes hypertension?",
    "How do you treat type 2 diabetes?"
]
responses = inference.batch_generate(questions)
```

Key features of the inference script:

- Supports both local and HuggingFace hosted models
- Includes 4-bit quantization for efficient memory usage
- Provides both single and batch inference
- Allows customization of generation parameters (temperature, top_p, etc.)
- Handles prompt formatting automatically
- Includes proper error handling and device management

Tips for optimal inference of DeepSeek models:

Adjust generation parameters:

- Lower temperature (0.3-0.5) for more focused responses
- Higher temperature (0.7-0.9) for more creative responses
- Adjust max_new_tokens based on your needs

Memory optimization:

- Use 4-bit quantization (load_in_4bit=True)
- Adjust batch_size based on your GPU memory
- Use gradient_checkpointing for longer sequences

Chapter 7: Designing AI Agents with DeepSeek R1

What are AI Agents?

Artificial Intelligence (AI) agents are autonomous entities designed to perceive their environment, process information, and take actions to achieve specific goals. They operate based on predefined rules, learned behaviors, or a combination of both, enabling them to perform tasks ranging from simple responses to complex problem-solving.

Types of AI Agents

AI agents are categorized based on their complexity and functionality:

- **Simple Reflex Agents**: These agents act solely based on the current percept, ignoring the rest of the percept history. They operate on condition-action rules, making them suitable for fully observable environments.
- **Model-Based Reflex Agents**: Building upon simple reflex agents, these agents maintain an internal model of the world, allowing them to handle partially observable environments by considering the history of percepts.
- **Goal-Based Agents**: These agents utilize goal information to make decisions, evaluating different actions to determine the ones that achieve their objectives. This approach enables them to plan and act beyond immediate responses.
- **Utility-Based Agents**: Beyond achieving goals, these agents assess the desirability of different states using a utility function, allowing them to make decisions that maximize their overall satisfaction or performance.

- **Learning Agents**: These agents have the capability to learn from experiences, improving their performance over time by adapting to new situations and refining their decision-making processes.

How DeepSeek R1 Enhances Agent Capabilities

DeepSeek R1, as an advanced large language model, significantly enhances AI agent capabilities through:

- **Advanced Reasoning**: Its sophisticated reasoning abilities enable agents to handle complex tasks, such as natural language understanding and problem-solving, with greater accuracy.
- **Cost Efficiency**: DeepSeek R1 offers high performance at a lower cost compared to some leading models, making it an attractive choice for enterprises aiming to maximize their AI investments.
- **Open-Source Flexibility**: Being open-source, DeepSeek R1 provides transparency and flexibility, fostering collaboration and innovation within the AI community.

Examples of AI Agents in Various Domains

AI agents are utilized across multiple industries:

- **Customer Service**: Chatbots and virtual assistants handle inquiries, provide information, and resolve issues, enhancing customer engagement and support efficiency.
- **Healthcare**: Diagnostic agents assist in analyzing medical data, supporting healthcare professionals in decision-making and patient care.
- **Finance**: Automated trading agents analyze market trends and execute trades, optimizing investment strategies.
- **Manufacturing**: Robotic agents manage assembly lines, monitor quality control, and adapt to changes in production processes.
- **Education**: Tutoring agents provide personalized learning experiences, adapting to individual student needs and progress.

The integration of models like DeepSeek R1 into AI agents across these domains enhances their ability to perform complex tasks efficiently and effectively.

Designing AI Agents with DeepSeek R1

Designing AI agents with DeepSeek R1 involves a systematic approach to integrate advanced language understanding and reasoning capabilities into autonomous systems.

Step-by-Step Guide to Building an AI Agent

1. **Define Objectives**: Clearly outline the tasks and goals the agent is expected to achieve.
2. **Select the Appropriate Agent Type**: Choose the type of agent (e.g., goal-based, utility-based) that aligns with the objectives.
3. **Develop the Agent Architecture**: Design the structural framework, including data flow, decision-making processes, and interaction mechanisms.
4. **Integrate DeepSeek R1**: Incorporate DeepSeek R1 to enhance language processing and reasoning capabilities.
5. **Implement APIs and External Tools**: Connect the agent to necessary external systems and databases through APIs to access and process relevant information.
6. **Build Conversational Interfaces**: Develop user interfaces that facilitate natural language interactions, leveraging DeepSeek R1's capabilities for understanding and generating human-like responses.
7. **Test and Iterate**: Conduct thorough testing to identify and address issues, refining the agent's performance through iterative improvements.

Integrating DeepSeek R1 with APIs and External Tools

To enhance the agent's functionality:

- **API Integration**: Utilize APIs to enable the agent to retrieve and process data from external sources, such as databases, web services, or other applications.
- **Tool Integration**: Incorporate tools for tasks like data analysis, content management, or workflow automation to expand the agent's capabilities.

Building Conversational Interfaces

For effective user interactions:

- **Natural Language Processing**: Leverage DeepSeek R1's language understanding to interpret user inputs accurately.
- **Dialogue Management**: Implement systems to manage the flow of conversation, ensuring coherent and contextually appropriate responses.

- **User Experience Design**: Focus on creating intuitive and user-friendly interfaces that facilitate seamless interactions.

Designing Reasoning-Powered Agents

Enhancing AI agents with reasoning capabilities allows them to handle complex tasks and make informed decisions.

Agent Frameworks: Autogen, CrewAI, LangGraph

These frameworks provide structures for developing reasoning-powered agents:

- **Autogen**: Facilitates the creation of autonomous agents capable of self-improvement through learning and adaptation.
- **CrewAI**: Enables collaborative reasoning among multiple agents, allowing them to work together to solve complex problems.
- **LangGraph**: Integrates language understanding with graph-based reasoning, enabling agents to process and analyze complex relational data.

Integrating Tools: Search APIs, Code Execution, Knowledge Bases

To empower agents with comprehensive reasoning abilities:

- **Search APIs**: Allow agents to access and retrieve information from various sources in real-time.
- **Code Execution**: Enables agents to run code, analyze outputs, and refine solutions dynamically.
- **Knowledge Bases**: Provide structured repositories of information that agents can reference to enhance their decision-making processes.

For further architectures, step by step lesson and full code samples of building AI Agents, check out my book, "The Complete LangGraph Blueprint: Build 50+ AI Agents for Business Success" available on exclusively Amazon.com

Using Groq API for High-Speed Reasoning

Reasoning models excel at complex problem-solving tasks that require step-by-step analysis, logical deduction, and structured thinking. With Groq inference speed, these types of models can deliver instant reasoning capabilities critical for real-time applications.

Why Speed Matters for Reasoning

Reasoning models require explicit reasoning chains as part of their token output. These chains build on previous results, making low-latency inference essential. Faster response times enable AI agents to provide real-time reasoning outputs, improving decision-making efficiency.

Supported Model

Model ID	Model
deepseek-r1-distill-llama-70b	DeepSeek R1 (Distil-Llama 70B)

Reasoning Format

Groq API supports explicit reasoning formats through the reasoning_format parameter, allowing for fine-grained control over the model's reasoning process:

reasoning_format Options	Description
parsed	Separates reasoning into a dedicated field while keeping the response concise.
raw	Includes reasoning within <think> tags in the content.
hidden	Returns only the final answer for maximum efficiency.

Quick Start with Groq API

```
from groq import Groq

client = Groq()
completion = client.chat.completions.create(
    model="deepseek-r1-distill-llama-70b",
    messages=[
        {
            "role": "user",
            "content": "How many r's are in the word strawberry?"
        }
    ],
    temperature=0.6,
    max_completion_tokens=1024,
    top_p=0.95,
    stream=True,
    reasoning_format="raw"
)
```

```
for chunk in completion:
    print(chunk.choices[0].delta.content or "", end="")
```

Output:

<think>

Okay, so I need to figure out how many times the letter 'r' appears in the word "strawberry." Hmm, let me think about this step by step. First, I should probably write out the word and then go through each letter one by one to count the 'r's.

Alright, the word is S-T-R-A-W-B-E-R-R-Y. Wait, let me make sure I have the spelling right. Sometimes I get confused with the double letters. I think it's S-T-R-A-W-B-E-R-R-Y. Yeah, that sounds right. So, let me write that down: S, T, R, A, W, B, E, R, R, Y. So that's 10 letters in total.

Now, I need to go through each letter and count how many times 'R' appears. Starting from the beginning:

1. S – not an R.
2. T – not an R.
3. R – that's one R.
4. A – not an R.
5. W – not an R.
6. B – not an R.
7. E – not an R.
8. R – that's the second R.
9. R – and that's the third R.
10. Y – not an R.

Wait, so I counted three R's. But I'm a bit confused because sometimes in words like "strawberry," people might think there are only two R's. Let me double-check. Maybe I'm overcounting.

Let me write the word again more carefully: S-T-R-A-W-B-E-R-R-Y. So after E, there are two R's in a row. So that's two R's there, and then one R earlier in the word. So that makes a total of three R's. Hmm, but I've heard some people say there are only two. Maybe I'm mistaken.

Wait, let me check the spelling again. The word is spelled S-T-R-A-W-B-E-R-R-Y. So the letters are S, T, R, A, W, B, E, R, R, Y. So yes, that's three R's. The first R is after T, then after E there are two more R's. So that makes three in total.

But I'm a bit unsure because sometimes when I say the word out loud, it doesn't feel like there are three R's. Maybe I'm just mishearing it. Let me try to pronounce it slowly: "straw-berry." So after "straw" comes "ber-ry." So in "berry," there's one R, but since it's "strawberry," maybe it's "straw" plus "berry," which has two R's. Wait, no, "berry" is B-E-R-R-Y, which has two R's. So when combined with "straw," does that make three R's in total?

Wait, no. Let me think again. "Straw" is S-T-R-A-W, so that's one R. Then "berry" is B-E-R-R-Y, which has two R's. So when you put them together, it's S-T-R-A-W-B-E-R-R-Y, which should have three R's. So I think I was right the first time. There are three R's in "strawberry."

But I'm still a bit confused because I've seen some sources say there are only two. Maybe I should look it up, but since I can't right now, I'll have to rely on my spelling. Let me count again: S (1), T (2), R (3), A (4), W (5), B (6), E (7), R (8), R (9), Y (10). So the R's are at positions 3, 8, and 9. That's three R's.

I think I must have been correct initially. So the answer should be three R's in the word "strawberry."
</think>

The word "strawberry" contains three 'r's.

Step-by-step explanation:
1. Spell out the word: S-T-R-A-W-B-E-R-R-Y.
2. Identify each letter and its position.
3. Count the occurrences of 'R':
   - Position 3: R
   - Position 8: R
   - Position 9: R
4. Total count: 3.

Additional use cases, with a practical viewpoint

Medical Symptom Analysis:

```
from groq import Groq

client = Groq()
completion = client.chat.completions.create(
    model="deepseek-r1-distill-llama-70b",
    messages=[
        {
            "role": "user",
            "content": "Patient presents with: fever, joint pain, and rash. What are potential diagnoses to consider?"
        }
    ],
    temperature=0.6,
    max_completion_tokens=1024,
    top_p=0.95,
    stream=True,
    reasoning_format="raw"
)

for chunk in completion:
    print(chunk.choices[0].delta.content or "", end="")
```

Output:
<think>

Okay, so I have a patient who's come in with fever, joint pain, and a rash. I need to figure out what could be causing these symptoms. Let me start by thinking about each symptom individually and then how they might connect.

Fever is a common symptom in many conditions, so that's pretty broad. It could be an infection, inflammation, or even something autoimmune. Joint pain makes me think of arthritis or maybe something like Lyme disease. The rash could be viral, bacterial, or allergic in nature.

I should consider infections first. Viral exanthems are a possibility since many viruses cause rashes along with fever. For example, measles or chickenpox, though those are usually pretty distinctive. Then there's Lyme disease, which is caused by a tick bite. The rash in Lyme is often a bullseye, and it can cause joint pain and fever. Rocky Mountain Spotted Fever is another tick-borne illness that presents with fever, rash, and sometimes joint pain.

Bacterial infections could also be the culprit. Scarlet fever comes to mind, which is caused by strep throat. It has a distinctive rash and fever. Staph or strep infections can cause skin infections like cellulitis or abscesses, which might present with a rash and fever, and maybe joint pain if it's related to an infected joint.

When thinking about autoimmune or inflammatory conditions, juvenile idiopathic arthritis (JIA) is a possibility, especially in children. It can cause joint pain, fever, and sometimes a rash. Lupus is another autoimmune disease that can present with a malar rash, fever, and joint pain, though it's more common in adults.

Allergic reactions could also cause a rash and fever, maybe from a drug reaction or an allergy to something else. The joint pain might be secondary or part of a more systemic reaction.

I shouldn't forget about zoonotic diseases like erythema migrans from Lyme disease, or maybe something like parvovirus B19, which causes fifth disease. That's a viral infection with a slapped-cheek rash and can have joint pain, especially in adults.

I should also consider the patient's history. Have they been bitten by ticks? Have they traveled recently? Are they immunocompromised? These factors can help narrow down the possibilities.

In terms of evaluation, I'd probably start with a thorough history and physical. Look for the characteristics of the rash—its appearance, location, whether it's spreading. Check the joints for swelling or redness. Maybe some labs like CBC, CRP, ESR to check for inflammation or infection. Depending on the history, maybe a Lyme titer or other specific tests.

Treatment would depend on the diagnosis. If it's bacterial, antibiotics. If it's viral, supportive care. For autoimmune conditions, maybe steroids or other immunosuppressants.

I should make sure I'm not missing anything rare but serious, like meningitis or sepsis, though those usually present with more severe symptoms. Also, consider if the rash is part of a more severe allergic reaction, like anaphylaxis, though that usually includes respiratory symptoms too.

So, putting it all together, the potential diagnoses could range from infections (viral, bacterial, tick-borne) to autoimmune conditions, allergic reactions, and maybe even something like Kawasaki disease, especially in children, which can cause fever, rash, and joint issues.

I think I've covered the main possibilities, but I should probably look up each condition to make sure I'm not missing any key features or tests needed.
</think>

The patient presenting with fever, joint pain, and rash could be experiencing one of several conditions. Here's a structured approach to potential diagnoses and considerations:

Potential Diagnoses:
1. **Infections:**
  - **Viral Exanthems:** Such as measles or chickenpox, though these often have distinctive features.
  - **Lyme Disease:** A tick-borne illness with a bullseye rash, joint pain, and fever.
  - **Rocky Mountain Spotted Fever:** Another tick-borne disease with fever, rash, and possible joint pain.
  - **Bacterial Infections:** Scarlet fever (from strep throat), or skin infections like cellulitis.

2. **Autoimmune/Inflammatory Conditions:**
  - **Juvenile Idiopathic Arthritis (JIA):** Especially in children, causing joint pain, fever, and rash.
  - **Systemic Lupus Erythematosus (SLE):** Presents with a malar rash, fever, and joint pain, more common in adults.

3. **Allergic Reactions:**
  - Drug reactions or allergies causing rash and fever, with possible secondary joint pain.

4. **Zoonotic Diseases:**
  - **Parvovirus B19:** Causes fifth disease with a slapped-cheek rash and joint pain, especially in adults.

5. **Other Considerations:**
  - **Kawasaki Disease:** Particularly in children

Legal Document Analysis:

```
from groq import Groq

client = Groq()
completion = client.chat.completions.create(
    model="deepseek-r1-distill-llama-70b",
    messages=[
        {
            "role": "user",
            "content": "Review this contract clause for potential risks: 'Party A shall make best efforts to deliver services within the specified timeframe."
        }
    ],
    temperature=0.6,
    max_completion_tokens=2048,
    top_p=0.95,
    stream=True,
    reasoning_format="raw"
)

for chunk in completion:
    print(chunk.choices[0].delta.content or "", end="")
```

Output:

<think>
Okay, so I need to review this contract clause: 'Party A shall make best efforts to deliver services within the specified timeframe.' I'm not very experienced with legal stuff, but I'll try to break it down step by step.

First, I know that contracts are important because they outline the responsibilities and expectations of both parties. So, this clause is about Party A delivering services on time. The phrase "best efforts" catches my eye. I think it means that Party A is supposed to try their hardest, but I'm not entirely sure how that's defined legally.

I remember hearing that some terms in contracts can be a bit vague. "Best efforts" might be one of those. It doesn't set a strict requirement, so maybe it's not as binding as saying "shall deliver." If Party A just has to try, what happens if they don't meet the timeframe? It seems like there's room for interpretation here. If things go wrong, how will anyone measure whether Party A actually made their best effort?

Also, the clause mentions a "specified timeframe," but I don't see any details about what happens if the delivery is late. Are there penalties? What recourse does the other party have? Without specific consequences, Party A might not have much incentive to stick to the timeline, especially if they're only obligated to try.

Another thought: what if the timeframe is unrealistic? If Party A agrees to a tight schedule and then can't meet it, how does that affect their liability? The clause doesn't say anything about flexibility or extensions. Maybe it should include some conditions under which the timeframe can be adjusted.

I also wonder about the quality of the services. The clause focuses on the timeframe, but what about the standard of work? If Party A rushes to meet the deadline, might the quality suffer? There's no mention of maintaining certain standards, which could be a problem if the services aren't up to par.

I should consider how enforceable this clause is. Since it's based on effort rather than results, it might be hard to take legal action if things go south. Courts might look at whether the effort was reasonable, but that's subjective. This could lead to disputes that are difficult and costly to resolve.

Maybe the clause should be more specific. Instead of "best efforts," it could outline measurable objectives or a clear deadline with consequences for missing it. That would make the expectations clearer for both parties and reduce the risk of misunderstandings.

I'm also thinking about force majeure or unforeseen circumstances. The clause doesn't mention anything about that. If something beyond Party A's control happens, like a natural disaster or a pandemic, are they still obligated to deliver on time? Without such a clause, Party A might still be held responsible, which isn't fair.

In terms of risk management, this clause could leave Party B vulnerable. If the services are crucial and the delivery is delayed without penalties, Party B might face their own losses without any compensation. It would be better to have some safeguards in place, like penalties or the option to terminate the contract if the timeframe isn't met.

I also think about how this affects the relationship between the parties. If Party A consistently misses deadlines without consequences, it could strain the partnership. Having clear terms might help maintain trust and cooperation.

So, to sum up, the main issues I see are the vagueness of "best efforts," lack of consequences for missing the timeframe, no mention of service quality, enforceability concerns, and absence of provisions for unforeseen events. Each of these points could pose risks, especially for Party B, if not properly addressed in the contract.
</think>

The contract clause 'Party A shall make best efforts to deliver services within the specified timeframe' presents several potential risks and areas for improvement:

1. **Vagueness of "Best Efforts":** The term "best efforts" is subjective and lacks a clear legal definition, making it difficult to enforce. It does not impose a strict obligation on Party A to meet the deadline.

2. **Lack of Consequences:** The clause does not specify penalties or recourse for missing the timeframe, potentially reducing Party A's incentive to adhere to the timeline.

3. **Unrealistic Timeframes:** The absence of flexibility in the timeframe may lead to issues if the schedule is unrealistic, potentially affecting Party A's liability.

4. **Quality of Services:** There is no mention of service quality, which could suffer if Party A rushes to meet the deadline.

5. **Enforceability Concerns:** The subjective nature of "best efforts" may lead to disputes that are difficult and costly to resolve legally.

6. **Force Majeure:** The clause lacks provisions for unforeseen events, potentially holding Party A responsible for circumstances beyond their control.

7. **Risk Management for Party B:** Without safeguards like penalties or termination options, Party B may face losses if services are delayed.

8. **Impact on Relationship:** Vague terms could strain the relationship between Party A and Party B if deadlines are consistently missed.

Recommendations:
- Replace "best efforts" with specific, measurable objectives.
- Include penalties for missing deadlines and consequences for subpar quality.
- Add provisions for adjusting the timeframe and addressing unforeseen events.
- Outline clear quality standards and consequences for non-compliance.

These changes would enhance clarity, enforceability, and fairness, protecting both parties' interests.

Financial Market Analysis:

```
from groq import Groq

client = Groq()
completion = client.chat.completions.create(
    model="deepseek-r1-distill-llama-70b",
    messages=[
        {
            "role": "user",
            "content": "Analyze the impact of rising interest rates on tech sector
stocks, considering historical patterns."
        }
```

```
    ],
    temperature=0.6,
    max_completion_tokens=2048,
    top_p=0.95,
    stream=True,
    reasoning_format="raw"
)

for chunk in completion:
    print(chunk.choices[0].delta.content or "", end="")
```

Output:

<think>

Okay, so I need to figure out how rising interest rates affect tech sector stocks by looking at historical patterns. I'm not entirely sure where to start, but I'll try to break it down step by step.

First, I remember that interest rates can influence the stock market. When rates go up, it probably affects different sectors in different ways. I think tech companies might be more sensitive because they often rely on borrowing money for things like research and development or expanding their operations. So, higher interest rates could make it more expensive for them to borrow, which might hurt their profitability. That makes sense because if it costs more to borrow, their expenses go up, and maybe their profits go down.

I also recall that tech companies sometimes have high valuations based on future growth expectations. So, when interest rates rise, the value of those future earnings might be discounted more because the discount rate (which is related to interest rates) increases. This could make their stock prices drop because investors are valuing future cash flows less.

Looking at historical examples, I think about the dot-com bubble in the late 90s and early 2000s. I remember that when the Fed raised rates back then, it might have contributed to the burst of the bubble. Tech stocks were overvalued, and higher rates made investors rethink how much they were willing to pay for future growth. That seems like a clear historical pattern where rising rates led to a decline in tech stocks.

Then there's the period after the 2008 financial crisis. The Fed kept rates low for a long time, and tech stocks did really well. This might be because low rates made borrowing cheap, and the tech sector could invest in growth without worrying about high interest expenses. So, when rates started to rise again in 2015-2018, I think the tech sector, especially the FAANG stocks, saw some volatility. Investors were concerned about the impact of higher rates on these companies' valuations. However, some big tech firms have strong cash reserves, which might have helped them weather the storm better than smaller companies.

More recently, during the COVID-19 pandemic, rates were cut to near zero, and tech stocks surged. This makes sense because the low rates made future cash flows more valuable, and investors flocked to tech as they expected strong growth. Now, with rates rising again to combat inflation, tech stocks, especially those with high valuations, are under pressure. I've heard that growth stocks are particularly sensitive to rate increases because their value is based more on future growth rather than current earnings.

I should also consider how interest rates affect the broader economy. Higher rates can slow down economic growth, which might reduce consumer and business spending on technology. If people and companies are spending less, tech companies might see reduced demand for their products and services, leading to lower revenues and profits.

Another angle is the impact on the cost of capital. Tech companies often invest in innovation and expansion, which requires capital. If the cost of borrowing increases, they might scale back investments, which could hinder their growth. This could make investors less optimistic about their future prospects, leading to a drop in stock prices.

I also wonder about the difference between established tech companies and startups. Big companies like Apple or Microsoft might have more cash reserves and established revenue streams, so they might be less affected by rising rates. On the other hand, startups that rely heavily on venture capital and borrowing might struggle more as the cost of capital increases. This could lead to a split where bigger tech firms are more resilient while smaller ones face more challenges.

Looking at the current situation, with central banks raising rates to fight inflation, tech stocks have been underperforming. This aligns with the historical pattern where rising rates make tech stocks less attractive compared to sectors with more stable earnings and higher dividends. Investors might be moving their money to more defensive sectors or to bonds that offer higher yields now.

I should also think about the long-term versus short-term effects. In the short term, rising rates can cause a sell-off in tech stocks as investors adjust their valuations. But in the long term, if the economy remains strong and tech companies can maintain their growth, they might recover. However, if higher rates lead to an economic slowdown, that could have a more prolonged negative impact on the sector.

I'm trying to piece together how all these factors interact. It seems like rising interest rates create a challenging environment for tech stocks, especially those dependent on growth and high valuations. Historical examples support this, showing that when rates go up, tech stocks tend to struggle, at least in the short to medium term.

I should also consider other factors that might influence this relationship. For example, the overall health of the economy, inflation levels, and the specific business models of tech companies can all play a role. But the overarching theme seems to be that rising rates increase borrowing costs, reduce the present value of future earnings, and can lead to decreased investment and consumer spending on technology.

In summary, my understanding is that rising interest rates typically have a negative impact on tech sector stocks, especially those with high valuations and growth-dependent models. Historical patterns from the dot-com burst, post-2008 recovery, and recent COVID-19 pandemic support this, showing that as rates rise, tech stocks often decline or underperform the market.
</think>

Rising interest rates have a multifaceted impact on the tech sector, particularly on stocks, as evidenced by historical patterns. Here's a structured summary of the analysis:

1. **Impact on Borrowing Costs**: Tech companies often rely on borrowing for R&D and expansion. Rising interest rates increase these borrowing costs, potentially reducing profitability and making it more expensive for companies to invest in growth.

2. **Valuation Effects**: Higher interest rates increase the discount rate used to value future cash flows, making them less valuable in the present. This particularly affects tech companies with high valuations based on future growth expectations, leading to stock price declines.

3. **Historical Context**:
 - **Dot-Com Bubble (Late 90s/Early 2000s)**: Rising rates contributed to the burst, as investors reevaluated high valuations.
 - **Post-2008 Recovery**: Low rates fueled tech growth, but subsequent rate hikes (2015-2018) caused volatility, especially in growth stocks.
 - **COVID-19 Pandemic**: Low rates led to a tech surge, but recent rate hikes have pressured the sector, particularly growth stocks.

4. **Economic Impact**: Higher rates can slow economic growth, reducing spending on technology, thus impacting revenues and profits for tech companies.

5. **Cost of Capital**: Increased borrowing costs may lead tech companies to scale back investments, potentially hindering growth and investor optimism.

6. **Sector Differences**: Established tech firms with strong cash reserves may be more resilient, while startups reliant on capital may struggle more.

7. **Current Trends**: Recent rate hikes have led to tech underperformance, with investors favoring sectors with stable earnings or higher-yield bonds.

8. **Long-Term vs. Short-Term Effects**: Short-term sell-offs may occur, but long-term impacts depend on economic strength and company growth sustainability.

In conclusion, rising interest rates typically create a challenging environment for tech stocks, especially those dependent on growth and high valuations. Historical patterns indicate that such stocks may decline or underperform during rate hikes, influenced by factors like borrowing costs, valuation changes, and economic conditions.

Chess Move Analysis:

```
from groq import Groq

client = Groq()
completion = client.chat.completions.create(
    model="deepseek-r1-distill-llama-70b",
    messages=[
        {
            "role": "user",
            "content": "In this position: e4 e5 Nf3 Nc6 Bb5, analyze Black's best response."
        }
    ],
    temperature=0.6,
    max_completion_tokens=2048,
    top_p=0.95,
    stream=True,
    reasoning_format="raw"
)

for chunk in completion:
    print(chunk.choices[0].delta.content or "", end="")
```

Output:

<think>

Alright, so I'm trying to figure out the best response for Black in this chess position: 1. e4 e5 2. Nf3 Nc6 3. Bb5. Hmm, okay, so this is the Ruy Lopez opening, right? I remember that the Ruy Lopez is one of the oldest and most popular openings, and it starts with these moves.

So, after 3. Bb5, Black has a few options. The main lines I can think of are 3...a6, 3...Nf6, and maybe 3...d6 or something else. I'm not entirely sure which one is the best, so I need to analyze each possibility.

First, let me consider 3...a6. This move challenges the bishop on b5 and aims to push it away. After 4.Ba4, Black can play 4...b5, attacking the bishop again. Then White might retreat the bishop to b3, and Black could respond with 5...c6. This seems like the Morphy Defense, which is a solid choice, but I'm not sure if it's the best.

Another option is 3...Nf6. This move develops the knight and prepares to develop other pieces. After 4.0-0, Black can castle kingside as well, leading to a position where both sides have their kings safe. This is the Berlin Defense, I think. It's known for being solid but maybe a bit passive.

I've also heard of the Classical Defense, which is 3...Bc5. This move develops the bishop and puts pressure on the e4 pawn. However, I'm not sure if this is the best because White can respond with 4.c3, preparing to push d4 and gain space in the center.

Then there's 3...d6, which is the Steinitz Defense. This move supports the e5 pawn and prepares to develop the dark-squared bishop. But I've read that this isn't the best because it can lead to a weaker pawn structure after White plays d4.

So, considering all these options, the main choices are 3...a6, 3...Nf6, and 3...Bc5. The Berlin Defense with 3...Nf6 seems solid but might lead to a drawish position. The Morphy Defense with 3...a6 is aggressive and can lead to sharp play. The Classical Defense with 3...Bc5 is also solid but might not be as popular as the other two.

I think the most aggressive and popular response is 3...a6, leading to the Morphy Defense. It challenges the bishop immediately and can lead to a lot of tactical play. However, some players prefer the Berlin Defense because it's more straightforward and leads to a solid structure.

I should also consider the current trends and what top players are choosing. From what I've seen, 3...a6 is still the most common response, but 3...Nf6 is also popular, especially in certain lines. The Classical Defense is less common but still a valid option.

In conclusion, after analyzing the options, I think the best responses for Black are either 3...a6 or 3...Nf6. Both have their pros and cons, but 3...a6 is more aggressive, while 3...Nf6 is more solid. Depending on Black's style, either could be a good choice.

</think>

In the position after 3. Bb5, Black has several options, but the most popular and aggressive response is **3...a6**, leading to the Morphy Defense. This move challenges the bishop and can result in sharp tactical play. Alternatively, **3...Nf6**, the Berlin Defense, is a solid choice for those preferring a more straightforward and stable game. Both moves are viable, with the choice depending on Black's strategic preferences.

Best response: 3...a6 or 3...Nf6

Code Debug Assistant

```
from groq import Groq

client = Groq()
completion = client.chat.completions.create(
    model="deepseek-r1-distill-llama-70b",
    messages=[
        {
            "role": "user",
            "content": """
        Debug this function:
        def fibonacci(n):
            if n <= 0:
                return []
            sequence = [0, 1]
            while len(sequence) < n:
                sequence.append(sequence[-1] + sequence[-2])
            return sequence
        """
        }
    ],
    temperature=0.6,
    max_completion_tokens=2048,
    top_p=0.95,
    stream=True,
    reasoning_format="raw"
)

for chunk in completion:
    print(chunk.choices[0].delta.content or "", end="")
```

Each example demonstrates different aspects of the Groq reasoning model:

- Different temperature settings for varying levels of creativity vs. determinism
- Use of both parsed and raw reasoning formats depending on the use case
- Streaming vs. non-streaming responses
- Various token limits based on expected response complexity
- Different top_p values for controlling response diversity
- Application across diverse domains: medicine, law, finance, games, programming, and ethics

These examples showcase how the Groq API can be used for complex reasoning tasks while maintaining high-speed inference capabilities.

Chapter 8: Implementing a Reasoning AI Agent with ChatDeepSeek

Introduction

In this chapter, we will explore the integration of the DeepSeek API with LangChain to create a reasoning AI agent. We will build a simple "Hello World" agent, progress to a conversational agent, and finally implement an agent capable of utilizing external tools.

Prerequisites

Before we begin, ensure you have the following:

- **Python Environment**: Python 3.10 or later installed.
- **DeepSeek API Key**: Sign up for a DeepSeek account and obtain your API key.
- **LangChain DeepSeek Library**: Install the langchain-deepseek-official package.

You can install the necessary package using pip:

```
pip install -U langchain-deepseek-official langgraph
export DEEPSEEK_API_KEY="your-api-key"
```

1. Creating a Simple "Hello World" Agent

Let's start by creating a basic agent that responds with a "Hello, World!" message.

```
from langgraph.graph import Graph, END
from langchain_groq import ChatGroq
from typing import TypedDict, Annotated, Sequence
import operator

# Define our state type
class AgentState(TypedDict):
    messages: Annotated[Sequence[str], operator.add]
    next_step: str

# Create the model
llm = ChatGroq(
    model="deepseek-r1-distill-llama-70b",
    temperature=0.6,
    max_tokens=2048
)

# Define the chat node
def chat_node(state: AgentState) -> AgentState:
    # Get the last message
    message = state["messages"][-1]

    # Generate response
    response = llm.invoke(message)

    # Update state
    return {
        "messages": [response.content],
        "next_step": "end"
    }

# Create the workflow
workflow = Graph()

# Add the node
workflow.set_entry_point("chat")
workflow.add_node("chat", chat_node)

# Add the edge from chat to end
workflow.add_edge("chat", END)

# Compile the graph
app = workflow.compile()

# Run the graph
result = app.invoke({
```

```
    "messages": ["Hello, how are you?"],
    "next_step": "chat"
})
print(result)
```

Output:

{'messages': ["<think>\n\n</think>\n\nHello! I'm just a virtual assistant, so I don't have feelings, but I'm here and ready to help you with whatever you need. How are you doing? 😊"], 'next_step': 'end'}

Explanation:

State Management:

- We define AgentState as a TypedDict that contains two key pieces of information:
  - messages: A sequence of strings that stores the conversation messages
  - next_step: A string that determines the next node in our workflow
- The Annotated[Sequence[str], operator.add] syntax tells LangGraph how to combine messages when merging states

Node Definition:

- The chat_node function is our main processing unit that:
  - Takes the current state as input
  - Extracts the last message from the messages list
  - Uses the DeepSeek model to generate a response
  - Returns a new state with the response and sets next_step to "end"

Graph Construction:

- workflow = Graph() creates a new workflow graph
- workflow.add_node("chat", chat_node) adds our chat processing node
- workflow.add_edge("chat", END) connects the chat node to the end of the workflow
- app = workflow.compile() compiles the graph into an executable application

Execution Flow:

- When we invoke the app with a message:
  1. The message enters the graph at the "chat" node
  2. The chat node processes the message using the LLM
  3. The response is added to the state
  4. The workflow ends since we have a direct edge to END

Advantages of this Approach:

- Clear separation of state management and processing logic
- Explicit workflow definition through graph structure

- Easy to extend by adding more nodes and edges
- Built-in state tracking and management

2. Developing a Conversational Agent

Now, we will create a conversational agent that continuously interacts with the user, processing each input and responding accordingly.

```
from langgraph.graph import Graph, END
from langchain_groq import ChatGroq
from typing import TypedDict, Annotated, Sequence, List, Tuple
import operator
from langchain_core.messages import HumanMessage, AIMessage

# Create the model
llm = ChatGroq(
    model="deepseek-r1-distill-llama-70b",
    temperature=0.6,
    max_tokens=2048
)

class ConversationState(TypedDict):
    history: Annotated[List[Tuple[str, str]], operator.add]
    current_message: str
    next_step: str

def process_message(state: ConversationState) -> ConversationState:
    # Get conversation history and current message
    history = state["history"]
    message = state["current_message"]

    # Format messages for the model using proper message types
    formatted_messages = []
    for user_msg, ai_msg in history:
        formatted_messages.extend([
            HumanMessage(content=user_msg),
            AIMessage(content=ai_msg)
        ])

    # Add current message
    formatted_messages.append(HumanMessage(content=message))

    # Get response
    response = llm.invoke(formatted_messages)

    # Update state
    return {
        "history": [(message, response.content)],
```

```
        "current_message": "",
        "next_step": "wait_for_input"
    }

def should_continue(state: ConversationState) -> str:
    if state["current_message"].lower() in ["exit", "quit", ""]:
        return END
    return "process_message"

# Create the workflow
conversation_graph = Graph()

# Add nodes
conversation_graph.add_node("process_message", process_message)
conversation_graph.set_entry_point("process_message")

# Add conditional edges
conversation_graph.add_conditional_edges(
    "process_message",
    should_continue
)

# Compile the graph
conversation_app = conversation_graph.compile()

def run_conversation():
    # Initialize state
    state = {
        "history": [],
        "current_message": "",
        "next_step": "process_message"
    }

    print("Chat started. Type 'exit' or 'quit' to end the conversation.")

    while True:
        try:
            # Get user input
            user_message = input("You: ")

            # Update state with user message
            state["current_message"] = user_message

            # Run the graph
            new_state = conversation_app.invoke(state)

            # Update state for next iteration
            state = {
                "history": new_state["history"],
                "current_message": "",
                "next_step": "process_message"
            }
```

```
            # Check for exit
            if new_state["next_step"] == END:
                print("Conversation ended.")
                break

            # Print AI response (last message in history)
            if new_state["history"]:
                print(f"AI: {new_state['history'][-1][1]}")

        except Exception as e:
            print(f"Error occurred: {str(e)}")
            print("Please try again.")

if __name__ == "__main__":
    run_conversation()
```

How It Works

1. User enters a message
2. Message is added to conversation state
3. Graph processes message through defined workflow
4. AI generates response
5. Response is displayed to user
6. Loop continues until user exits

Key Features

- Maintains conversation history
- Proper message formatting for AI model
- Error handling
- Clean exit functionality
- State persistence between turns

3. Implementing Tool Use in the Agent – The real power of DeepSeek R1

We can now enable the agent to interact with external tools, such as retrieving weather data or population statistics. Sign up for a search API such as Tavily from https://tavily.com/ and setup the api key.

```
pip install -U langchain_community langchain_core langchain_groq langgraph
```

```
export TAVILY_API_KEY="your-api-key"
```

Then define the python file *tool-use.py* as below

```
from langgraph.graph import Graph, END
from langchain_groq import ChatGroq
from typing import TypedDict, Annotated, Sequence, List, Tuple, Dict, Any
import operator
from langchain_core.messages import HumanMessage, AIMessage, SystemMessage
from langchain_community.tools.tavily_search import TavilySearchResults
import json

# Create the model
llm = ChatGroq(
    model="deepseek-r1-distill-llama-70b",
    temperature=0.6,
    max_tokens=2048
)

# Initialize Tavily search tool with specific search type
search_tool = TavilySearchResults(
    max_results=3,
    include_raw_content=True,
    include_images=False,
    search_depth="advanced"
)

class ConversationState(TypedDict):
    history: Annotated[List[Tuple[str, str]], operator.add]
    current_message: str
    next_step: str
    needs_search: bool
    search_results: str

def perform_search(query: str) -> str:
    """Perform web search and return formatted results."""
    try:
        # Add specific search terms to improve results
        enhanced_query = f"current {query} specific factual information"
        search_results = search_tool.invoke(enhanced_query)

        # Format results with better structure
        formatted_results = []
        for result in search_results[:3]:  # Get top 3 results
            # Extract and clean the content
            content = result.get('content', '').strip()
            title = result.get('title', '').strip()
            url = result.get('url', '').strip()

            # Format each result
```

```
            formatted_result = f"Source: {title}\nContent: {content[:300]}...\nURL:
{url}\n"
            formatted_results.append(formatted_result)

        return "\n\n".join(formatted_results)
    except Exception as e:
        return f"Error performing search: {str(e)}"

def process_message(state: Dict[str, Any]) -> Dict[str, Any]:
    message = state["current_message"]
    history = state["history"]

    # Always perform search for messages that explicitly request it
    needs_search = "search" in message.lower() or "find" in message.lower() or "look
up" in message.lower()
    search_results = ""

    if needs_search:
        search_results = perform_search(message)

    # Format messages for the model
    formatted_messages = []

    # Add system message with context
    system_message = """You are a helpful assistant that can search the web for
current information.
    When search results are available, use them to provide accurate, up-to-date
information.
    Always cite your sources when using search results."""

    formatted_messages.append(SystemMessage(content=system_message))

    # Add search results if available
    if search_results:
        formatted_messages.append(SystemMessage(content=f"Search
Results:\n{search_results}"))

    # Add conversation history
    for user_msg, ai_msg in history:
        formatted_messages.extend([
            HumanMessage(content=user_msg),
            AIMessage(content=ai_msg)
        ])

    # Add current message
    formatted_messages.append(HumanMessage(content=message))

    # Get response
    response = llm.invoke(formatted_messages)

    return {
        "history": [(message, response.content)],
        "current_message": "",
```

```
        "next_step": "process_message",
        "needs_search": needs_search,
        "search_results": search_results
    }

def should_continue(state: Dict[str, Any]) -> str:
    if state["current_message"].lower() in ["exit", "quit", ""]:
        return END
    return "process_message"

# Create the workflow
workflow = Graph()
workflow.add_node("process_message", process_message)
workflow.set_entry_point("process_message")
workflow.add_conditional_edges("process_message", should_continue)
app = workflow.compile()

def run_conversation():
    state = {
        "history": [],
        "current_message": "",
        "next_step": "process_message",
        "needs_search": False,
        "search_results": ""
    }

    print("Chat started. Type 'exit' or 'quit' to end the conversation.")
    print("I can search the web for current information! Just ask me to search for
something.")
    print("Example: 'search for the weather in Nairobi' or 'find current news
about...'")

    while True:
        try:
            user_message = input("You: ")

            if user_message.lower() in ["exit", "quit", ""]:
                print("Conversation ended.")
                break

            state["current_message"] = user_message
            new_state = app.invoke(state)

            if new_state["history"]:
                if new_state.get("needs_search", False):
                    print("🔍 Searching the web for information...")
                print(f"AI: {new_state['history'][-1][1]}")

            state = {
                "history": new_state["history"],
                "current_message": "",
                "next_step": "process_message",
                "needs_search": False,
```

```
                "search_results": ""
            }

        except Exception as e:
            print(f"Error occurred: {str(e)}")
            print("Please try again.")

if __name__ == "__main__":
    run_conversation()
```

Output:

```
Chat started. Type 'exit' or 'quit' to end the conversation.
I can search the web for current information! Just ask me to search for something.
Example: 'search for the weather in Nairobi' or 'find current news about...'
You: search for the weather in Nairobi
🔍 Searching the web for information...
AI: <think>
Okay, so I need to figure out the weather in Nairobi right now and also what it's
expected to be like in January 2025. Let me start by looking at the sources provided.

First, the initial source from weatherapi.com gives the current weather in Nairobi as
of January 31, 2025, at 7:03 AM local time. The temperature is 15.1°C, which is about
59.18°F. It also mentions the location coordinates and time zone, which is helpful
for context.

Next, the second source from world-weather.info provides a detailed forecast for
January 2025. It shows that temperatures range from 77°F to 79°F (25°C to 26°C)
during the first few days, with the lowest temperatures around 63°F to 64°F (17°C to
18°C). This suggests that January is relatively warm in Nairobi, but with some cooler
days.

The third source, weather25.com, talks about the average weather in Nairobi during
January. It mentions that the weather can vary between cold and nice days, but the
specific temperatures aren't detailed there. It does provide a link for a 14-day
forecast, which might have more specific information, but I can't access that right
now.

Putting this all together, the current weather is mild, around 15°C, which is typical
for Nairobi's climate. For January 2025, the temperatures are expected to be warm
during the day and cooler at night, which aligns with Nairobi's subtropical highland
climate. It's important to note that while the sources agree on the general
temperature ranges, the exact numbers can vary slightly between sources.

I should also consider the time of data collection. The first source is current as of
January 31, 2025, so it's very up-to-date. The second source is a forecast, so it's
predictive but based on historical data. The third source is more general but still
relevant.

In summary, Nairobi's weather is mild currently and expected to stay warm in January
2025, with temperatures fluctuating between warmer days and cooler nights.
```

```
</think>

The current weather in Nairobi as of January 31, 2025, at 7:03 AM local time is
15.1°C (59.18°F). For January 2025, the forecast indicates warm daytime temperatures
ranging from 25°C to 26°C (77°F to 79°F), with cooler nights around 17°C to 18°C
(63°F to 64°F). This aligns with Nairobi's subtropical highland climate,
characterized by mild temperatures with variations between day and night.

Sources:
- WeatherAPI: Current weather as of January 31, 2025.
- World-Weather.info: Detailed forecast for January 2025.
- Weather25.com: General weather overview for January.
```

Explanation:

- We define tools using Pydantic models.
- These tools allow the agent to query external data sources for specific information.
- The agent can call these tools dynamically during execution.

4. Generating Structured Output

Instead of raw text responses, we can structure the AI output for more predictable and machine-readable results.

```
from langgraph.graph import Graph, END
from langchain_groq import ChatGroq
from typing import TypedDict, Annotated, Sequence, List, Tuple, Dict, Any, Optional
import operator
from langchain_core.messages import HumanMessage, AIMessage, SystemMessage
from langchain_community.tools.tavily_search import TavilySearchResults
from langchain_core.pydantic_v1 import BaseModel, Field
from datetime import datetime

class SearchResult(BaseModel):
    """Structure for search results"""
    title: str = Field(description="Title of the search result")
    content: str = Field(description="Main content from the source")
    url: str = Field(description="Source URL")
    relevance_score: Optional[float] = Field(description="How relevant the result is
to the query", ge=0, le=1)

class WeatherResponse(BaseModel):
    """Structure for weather responses"""
    location: str = Field(description="Location for the weather information")
    current_conditions: str = Field(description="Current weather conditions")
    temperature: Optional[str] = Field(description="Current temperature if
available")
    source: str = Field(description="Source of the weather information")
    last_updated: Optional[str] = Field(description="When this information was last
updated")
```

```
    confidence: float = Field(description="Confidence in the weather information",
ge=0, le=1)

class GeneralResponse(BaseModel):
    """Structure for general chat responses"""
    response_text: str = Field(description="Main response content")
    requires_search: bool = Field(description="Whether this response needed web
search")
    search_results: Optional[List[SearchResult]] = Field(description="Search results
if any were needed")
    confidence: float = Field(description="Confidence in the response", ge=0, le=1)

# Create the model
llm = ChatGroq(
    model="deepseek-r1-distill-llama-70b",
    temperature=0.6,
    max_tokens=2048
)

# Initialize structured output models
weather_model = llm.with_structured_output(WeatherResponse)
general_model = llm.with_structured_output(GeneralResponse)

# Initialize search tool
search_tool = TavilySearchResults(
    max_results=3,
    include_raw_content=True,
    search_depth="advanced"
)

class ConversationState(TypedDict):
    history: Annotated[List[Tuple[str, BaseModel]], operator.add]
    current_message: str
    next_step: str

def perform_search(query: str) -> List[SearchResult]:
    """Perform web search and return structured results."""
    try:
        raw_results = search_tool.invoke(query)
        search_results = []

        for result in raw_results[:3]:
            search_result = SearchResult(
                title=result.get('title', '').strip(),
                content=result.get('content', '').strip()[:300],
                url=result.get('url', '').strip(),
                relevance_score=0.8  # You could implement more sophisticated scoring
            )
            search_results.append(search_result)

        return search_results
    except Exception as e:
        return [SearchResult(
```

```
            title="Error",
            content=f"Error performing search: {str(e)}",
            url="",
            relevance_score=0.0
        )]

def is_weather_query(message: str) -> bool:
    """Determine if this is a weather-related query."""
    weather_terms = ["weather", "temperature", "forecast", "rain", "sunny",
"climate"]
    return any(term in message.lower() for term in weather_terms)

def process_message(state: ConversationState) -> ConversationState:
    """Process message and return structured response."""
    message = state["current_message"]

    # Handle weather queries
    if is_weather_query(message):
        # Perform weather-specific search
        search_results = perform_search(f"current weather {message}")

        if search_results:
            # Extract location from message
            location = message.lower().replace("weather", "").replace("in",
"").strip()

            response = weather_model.invoke(
                f"""Based on these search results, provide weather information for
{location}:
                {[result.content for result in search_results]}"""
            )
        else:
            response = WeatherResponse(
                location=location,
                current_conditions="Unable to fetch weather data",
                source="N/A",
                confidence=0.0
            )
    else:
        # Handle general queries
        needs_search = "search" in message.lower() or "find" in message.lower()
        search_results = perform_search(message) if needs_search else []

        response = general_model.invoke(
            message,
            {"search_results": search_results if search_results else None}
        )

    return {
        "history": [(message, response)],
        "current_message": "",
        "next_step": "process_message"
    }
```

```
def format_response(response: BaseModel) -> str:
    """Format the structured response for display."""
    if isinstance(response, WeatherResponse):
        output = [
            f"Weather Information for {response.location}:",
            f"Conditions: {response.current_conditions}"
        ]
        if response.temperature:
            output.append(f"Temperature: {response.temperature}")
        output.append(f"Source: {response.source}")
        output.append(f"Last Updated: {response.last_updated}")
        return "\n".join(output)

    elif isinstance(response, GeneralResponse):
        output = [response.response_text]
        if response.search_results:
            output.append("\nSources:")
            for result in response.search_results:
                output.append(f"- {result.title}: {result.url}")
        return "\n".join(output)

    return str(response)

def should_continue(state: ConversationState) -> str:
    """Determine if the conversation should continue."""
    if state["current_message"].lower() in ["exit", "quit", ""]:
        return END
    return "process_message"

# Create the workflow
workflow = Graph()
workflow.add_node("process_message", process_message)
workflow.set_entry_point("process_message")
workflow.add_conditional_edges("process_message", should_continue)
app = workflow.compile()

def run_conversation():
    """Run the conversation loop."""
    state = {
        "history": [],
        "current_message": "",
        "next_step": "process_message"
    }

    print("Chat started. Type 'exit' or 'quit' to end the conversation.")
    print("You can ask about:")
    print("- Weather (e.g., 'what's the weather in London?')")
    print("- Search for information (e.g., 'search for latest news about...')")

    while True:
        try:
            user_message = input("You: ")
```

```
            if user_message.lower() in ["exit", "quit", ""]:
                print("Conversation ended.")
                break

            state["current_message"] = user_message
            new_state = app.invoke(state)

            if new_state["history"]:
                _, response = new_state["history"][-1]
                print("\nAI:", format_response(response))

            state = {
                "history": new_state["history"],
                "current_message": "",
                "next_step": "process_message"
            }

        except Exception as e:
            print(f"Error occurred: {str(e)}")
            print("Please try again.")

if __name__ == "__main__":
    run_conversation()
```

Output:

Chat started. Type 'exit' or 'quit' to end the conversation.
You can ask about:
- Weather (e.g., 'what's the weather in London?')
- Search for information (e.g., 'search for latest news about...')
You: whats the weather in London?

AI: Weather Information for London, United Kingdom:
Conditions: High temperature around +46°C
Temperature: +46°C
Source: Historical Climate Data
Last Updated: 2025-01-31 17:36

Explanation:

- We define a structured output schema using Pydantic.
- The AI model returns responses formatted according to the schema.

5. Tracking Token Usage and Metadata

For performance monitoring and cost estimation, we can track the token usage and response metadata.

```
from langgraph.graph import Graph, END
```

```
from langchain_groq import ChatGroq
from typing import TypedDict, Annotated, Sequence, List, Tuple, Dict, Any, Optional
import operator
from langchain_core.messages import HumanMessage, AIMessage, SystemMessage
from langchain_core.pydantic_v1 import BaseModel, Field
import time
from datetime import datetime
import json

class PerformanceMetrics(BaseModel):
    """Structure for tracking performance metrics"""
    timestamp: str = Field(description="When the request was made")
    response_time: float = Field(description="Time taken to generate response in
seconds")
    input_tokens: int = Field(description="Number of input tokens")
    output_tokens: int = Field(description="Number of output tokens")
    total_tokens: int = Field(description="Total tokens used")
    cost_estimate: float = Field(description="Estimated cost in USD")
    success: bool = Field(description="Whether the request was successful")
    error: Optional[str] = Field(description="Error message if any")

class Response(BaseModel):
    """Structure for responses with performance tracking"""
    content: str = Field(description="The response content")
    metrics: PerformanceMetrics = Field(description="Performance metrics for this
response")

# Create the model
llm = ChatGroq(
    model="deepseek-r1-distill-llama-70b",
    temperature=0.6,
    max_tokens=2048
)

class ConversationState(TypedDict):
    history: Annotated[List[Tuple[str, Response]], operator.add]
    current_message: str
    next_step: str
    metrics: List[PerformanceMetrics]

def calculate_tokens(text: str) -> int:
    """Rough token count estimation"""
    return len(text.split()) * 1.3  # Rough approximation

def calculate_cost(input_tokens: int, output_tokens: int) -> float:
    """Calculate estimated cost in USD based on DeepSeek pricing"""
    # DeepSeek rates: $0.55 per 1M input tokens, $2.19 per 1M output tokens
    INPUT_RATE = 0.55 / 1_000_000  # per token
    OUTPUT_RATE = 2.19 / 1_000_000  # per token
    return (input_tokens * INPUT_RATE) + (output_tokens * OUTPUT_RATE)

def track_performance(func):
    """Decorator to track performance metrics"""
```

```
    def wrapper(*args, **kwargs):
        start_time = time.time()
        error = None

        try:
            result = func(*args, **kwargs)
            success = True
        except Exception as e:
            result = str(e)
            error = str(e)
            success = False

        end_time = time.time()
        response_time = end_time - start_time

        # Calculate token usage
        input_text = kwargs.get('message', '')
        output_text = result if isinstance(result, str) else str(result)
        input_tokens = int(calculate_tokens(input_text))
        output_tokens = int(calculate_tokens(output_text))

        metrics = PerformanceMetrics(
            timestamp=datetime.now().isoformat(),
            response_time=response_time,
            input_tokens=input_tokens,
            output_tokens=output_tokens,
            total_tokens=input_tokens + output_tokens,
            cost_estimate=calculate_cost(input_tokens, output_tokens),
            success=success,
            error=error
        )

        if success:
            return Response(content=result, metrics=metrics)
        else:
            raise Exception(error)

    return wrapper

@track_performance
def process_message(message: str) -> str:
    """Process a message and return response"""
    response = llm.invoke([HumanMessage(content=message)])
    return response.content

def log_metrics(metrics: PerformanceMetrics, log_file: str =
"performance_metrics.jsonl"):
    """Log performance metrics to a file"""
    with open(log_file, 'a') as f:
        f.write(json.dumps(metrics.dict()) + '\n')

def get_performance_summary(metrics_list: List[PerformanceMetrics]) -> Dict[str,
Any]:
```

```
    """Calculate summary statistics from metrics"""
    if not metrics_list:
        return {}

    total_requests = len(metrics_list)
    successful_requests = sum(1 for m in metrics_list if m.success)
    total_tokens = sum(m.total_tokens for m in metrics_list)
    total_cost = sum(m.cost_estimate for m in metrics_list)
    avg_response_time = sum(m.response_time for m in metrics_list) / total_requests

    return {
        "total_requests": total_requests,
        "successful_requests": successful_requests,
        "error_rate": (total_requests - successful_requests) / total_requests,
        "total_tokens_used": total_tokens,
        "total_cost_estimate": total_cost,
        "average_response_time": avg_response_time
    }

def process_with_state(state: Dict[str, Any]) -> Dict[str, Any]:
    """Process message with state management"""
    message = state["current_message"]

    try:
        response = process_message(message=message)

        # Log metrics
        log_metrics(response.metrics)

        # Update metrics history
        state["metrics"] = state.get("metrics", []) + [response.metrics]

        return {
            "history": [(message, response)],
            "current_message": "",
            "next_step": "process_message",
            "metrics": state["metrics"]
        }
    except Exception as e:
        print(f"Error: {str(e)}")
        return state

def format_metrics(metrics: PerformanceMetrics) -> str:
    """Format metrics for display"""
    # Calculate cost components for detailed breakdown
    input_cost = (metrics.input_tokens * 0.55) / 1_000_000
    output_cost = (metrics.output_tokens * 2.19) / 1_000_000
    total_cost = input_cost + output_cost

    return f"""
Performance Metrics:
- Response Time: {metrics.response_time:.2f}s
```

```
- Tokens Used: {metrics.total_tokens} (Input: {metrics.input_tokens}, Output:
{metrics.output_tokens})
- Cost Breakdown:
  • Input tokens: ${input_cost:.8f}
  • Output tokens: ${output_cost:.8f}
  • Total cost: ${total_cost:.8f}
- Status: {'✓' if metrics.success else 'X'}
"""

def should_continue(state: Dict[str, Any]) -> str:
    """Determine if conversation should continue"""
    if state["current_message"].lower() in ["exit", "quit", ""]:
        return END
    return "process_message"

# Create the workflow
workflow = Graph()
workflow.add_node("process_message", process_with_state)
workflow.set_entry_point("process_message")
workflow.add_conditional_edges("process_message", should_continue)
app = workflow.compile()

def run_conversation():
    """Run the conversation with performance tracking"""
    state = {
        "history": [],
        "current_message": "",
        "next_step": "process_message",
        "metrics": []
    }

    print("Chat started. Type 'exit' or 'quit' to end the conversation.")
    print("Type 'metrics' to see performance summary.")

    while True:
        try:
            user_message = input("You: ")

            if user_message.lower() == "metrics":
                summary = get_performance_summary(state["metrics"])
                print("\nPerformance Summary:")
                for key, value in summary.items():
                    print(f"{key}: {value}")
                continue

            if user_message.lower() in ["exit", "quit", ""]:
                print("\nFinal Performance Summary:")
                summary = get_performance_summary(state["metrics"])
                for key, value in summary.items():
                    print(f"{key}: {value}")
                print("\nConversation ended.")
                break
```

```
            state["current_message"] = user_message
            new_state = app.invoke(state)

            if new_state["history"]:
                _, response = new_state["history"][-1]
                print(f"\nAI: {response.content}")
                print(format_metrics(response.metrics))

            state = new_state

        except Exception as e:
            print(f"Error occurred: {str(e)}")
            print("Please try again.")

if __name__ == "__main__":
    run_conversation()
```

Output:

You: What is the capital of Kenya?

AI: <think>

</think>

The capital of Kenya is Nairobi.

Performance Metrics:
- Response Time: 0.34s
- Tokens Used: 17 (Input: 7, Output: 10)
- Cost Breakdown:
  • Input tokens: $0.00000385
  • Output tokens: $0.00002190
  • Total cost: $0.00002575
- Status: ✓

Explanation:

- The usage_metadata provides insights into how many tokens were used.
- The response_metadata may contain additional request details.

Conclusion

By integrating DeepSeek with LangChain, we have developed a series of AI agents—from a simple "Hello World" model to a conversational AI with memory, tool usage, structured output, and metadata tracking. These capabilities demonstrate the power of combining DeepSeek's efficient language model with LangChain's structured framework for building advanced AI applications.

For more details and advanced implementations, refer to the DeepSeek API documentation and LangChain tutorials.

Chapter 9: Creating Multi-Agent Reasoning Systems with DeepSeek

Introduction

Building on our previous exploration of single-agent systems, this chapter delves into creating multi-agent reasoning systems using DeepSeek and LangChain. We'll implement a collaborative system where multiple specialized agents work together to solve complex problems through structured communication and task delegation.

Prerequisites

Before beginning this chapter, ensure you have:
- Completed Chapter 8's implementations
- Updated dependencies:

```
pip install -U langchain_community langchain_core langchain_groq langgraph pydantic

export TAVILY_API_KEY="your-api-key"
export GROQ_API_KEY="your-api-key"
```

Designing the Multi-Agent Architecture

In this section, we explore a modular multi-agent system that leverages DeepSeek R1 to tackle complex tasks. The design features specialized agents that work in parallel, each handling a specific aspect of a larger problem. This architecture emphasizes robust inter-agent communication, task delegation, error handling, and performance monitoring.
Below, we break down the system into its main components, interspersed with the original code for clarity.

Agent Roles and Responsibilities

We'll create a system with four specialized agents:

- **Coordinator Agent**: Manages the overall workflow by receiving high-level tasks, decomposing them into subtasks, and delegating these subtasks to other agents.
- **Research Agent:** Gathers and verifies relevant information.
- **Analysis Agent:** Processes the gathered data and performs calculations
- **Integration Agent:** Combines the outputs from the Research and Analysis agents to generate the final, cohesive response.

1. Define an Inter-Agent Communication Protocol

A key element of this system is a standardized communication protocol. Agents exchange messages using a defined structure, ensuring consistency and clarity. The following code sets up the necessary modules and defines the *AgentMessage* and *AgentState* data structures.

```
import asyncio
from datetime import datetime
from typing import TypedDict, List, Dict, Any
from pydantic import BaseModel, Field
from abc import ABC, abstractmethod
from langchain_groq import ChatGroq
from langchain_core.messages import HumanMessage, AIMessage
import logging
import json
from rich.console import Console
from rich.logging import RichHandler

# Set up rich console for pretty printing
console = Console()

# Configure logging with rich handler
logging.basicConfig(
    level=logging.INFO,
```

```
    format="%(message)s",
    datefmt="[%X]",
    handlers=[RichHandler(rich_tracebacks=True, console=console)]
)
log = logging.getLogger("multi_agent")

class AgentMessage(BaseModel):
    """Structure for messages between agents"""
    sender: str = Field(description="ID of the sending agent")
    receiver: str = Field(description="ID of the receiving agent")
    message_type: str = Field(description="Type of message (task, response, query,
etc.)")
    content: Dict[str, Any] = Field(description="Message content")
    timestamp: str = Field(description="Time message was sent")
    priority: int = Field(description="Message priority (1-5)")
    requires_response: bool = Field(description="Whether message needs a response")

    def __str__(self):
        return json.dumps(self.dict(), indent=2)

class AgentState(TypedDict):
    """Structure for maintaining agent state"""
    agent_id: str
    current_task: Dict[str, Any]
    message_queue: List[AgentMessage]
    knowledge_base: Dict[str, Any]
    status: str
```

Explanation

- **Imports and Setup:** Modules like asyncio, datetime, and pydantic are imported for asynchronous programming, timestamping, and data validation respectively. The rich library is used for enhanced logging.
- **AgentMessage:** This class defines the schema for messages exchanged between agents. It includes sender/receiver IDs, message type, content, timestamp, and additional metadata.
- **AgentState:** A typed dictionary that maintains the current state of an agent, including its task, message queue, knowledge base, and status.

2. Implementing Base Agent Classes

All agents inherit from a common abstract class *BaseAgent*. This class provides shared functionality, such as logging and message sending, while enforcing the implementation of task-specific behaviors via abstract methods.

```
class BaseAgent(ABC):
    def __init__(self, agent_id: str, model: ChatGroq):
        self.agent_id = agent_id
        self.model = model
        self.state = AgentState(
```

```
            agent_id=agent_id,
            current_task={},
            message_queue=[],
            knowledge_base={},
            status="idle"
        )
        self.log = logging.getLogger(f"agent.{agent_id}")

    @abstractmethod
    async def process_message(self, message: AgentMessage) -> AgentMessage:
        """Process incoming message and generate response"""
        pass

    @abstractmethod
    async def perform_task(self, task: Dict[str, Any]) -> Dict[str, Any]:
        """Perform agent-specific task"""
        pass

    async def send_message(self, receiver: str, content: Dict[str, Any],
                           message_type: str = "task", priority: int = 3) ->
AgentMessage:
        """Send message to another agent"""
        message = AgentMessage(
            sender=self.agent_id,
            receiver=receiver,
            message_type=message_type,
            content=content,
            timestamp=datetime.now().isoformat(),
            priority=priority,
            requires_response=True
        )
        self.log.info(f"Sending message to {receiver}:\n{message}")
        return message

class CoordinatorAgent(BaseAgent):
    """Manages workflow and task delegation"""
    async def process_message(self, message: AgentMessage) -> AgentMessage:
        self.log.info(f"Processing message:\n{message}")

        if message.message_type == "task_request":
            self.log.info("Decomposing task into subtasks...")
            task_result = await self.perform_task(message.content)
            subtasks = task_result["subtasks"]
            self.log.info(f"Created subtasks:\n{json.dumps(subtasks, indent=2)}")

            for researcher_task in subtasks["researcher"]:
                await self.send_message("researcher",
                                        {"task": researcher_task},
                                        "research_request")

            for analyst_task in subtasks["analyst"]:
                await self.send_message("analyst",
                                        {"task": analyst_task},
```

```
                                     "analysis_request")

            return await self.send_message(
                "integrator",
                {"tasks": subtasks["integrator"]},
                "integration_request"
            )

        self.log.warning(f"Received unsupported message type:
{message.message_type}")
        return await self.send_message(
            message.sender,
            {"error": "Unsupported message type"},
            "error"
        )

    async def perform_task(self, task: Dict[str, Any]) -> Dict[str, Any]:
        """Implementation of abstract method for task execution"""
        self.log.info(f"Performing task: {task}")

        # Break down the main task into subtasks for each agent
        subtasks = {
            "researcher": [
                "Gather current research on AI in healthcare",
                "Collect case studies of successful AI healthcare implementations",
                "Research potential risks and limitations"
            ],
            "analyst": [
                "Analyze effectiveness of AI in different healthcare domains",
                "Evaluate cost-benefit ratios of AI healthcare solutions",
                "Identify emerging trends and patterns"
            ],
            "integrator": [
                "Compile findings into comprehensive report",
                "Generate actionable recommendations",
                "Create executive summary"
            ]
        }

        self.log.info(f"Created subtasks: {subtasks}")
        return {"subtasks": subtasks}

class ResearchAgent(BaseAgent):
    """Handles information gathering"""
    async def process_message(self, message: AgentMessage) -> AgentMessage:
        self.log.info(f"Processing research request: {message}")

        if message.message_type == "research_request":
            result = await self.perform_task(message.content)
            return await self.send_message(
                "integrator",
                {"research_results": result["findings"]},
                "research_results"
```

```
        )

        return await self.send_message(
            message.sender,
            {"error": "Unsupported message type"},
            "error"
        )

    async def perform_task(self, task: Dict[str, Any]) -> Dict[str, Any]:
        """Implementation of research task execution"""
        self.log.info(f"Performing research task: {task}")
        response = await self.model.ainvoke(
            [HumanMessage(content=f"Research this topic: {task['task']}")]
        )
        return {"findings": response.content}

class AnalysisAgent(BaseAgent):
    """Processes data and performs calculations"""
    async def process_message(self, message: AgentMessage) -> AgentMessage:
        self.log.info(f"Processing analysis request: {message}")

        if message.message_type == "analysis_request":
            result = await self.perform_task(message.content)
            return await self.send_message(
                "integrator",
                {"analysis_results": result["analysis"]},
                "analysis_results"
            )

        return await self.send_message(
            message.sender,
            {"error": "Unsupported message type"},
            "error"
        )

    async def perform_task(self, task: Dict[str, Any]) -> Dict[str, Any]:
        """Implementation of analysis task execution"""
        self.log.info(f"Performing analysis task: {task}")
        response = await self.model.ainvoke(
            [HumanMessage(content=f"Analyze this topic: {task['task']}")]
        )
        return {"analysis": response.content}

class IntegrationAgent(BaseAgent):
    """Combines outputs and generates final responses"""
    async def process_message(self, message: AgentMessage) -> AgentMessage:
        self.log.info(f"Processing integration request: {message}")

        if message.message_type == "integration_request":
            result = await self.perform_task(message.content)
            return await self.send_message(
                "system",
                {"response": result["integrated_response"]},
```

```
            "final_response"
        )
    elif message.message_type in ["research_results", "analysis_results"]:
        # Store results for later integration
        self.state.knowledge_base[message.message_type] = message.content
        if len(self.state.knowledge_base) >= 2:  # We have both research and
analysis
            result = await self.perform_task(self.state.knowledge_base)
            return await self.send_message(
                "system",
                {"response": result["integrated_response"]},
                "final_response"
            )

    return await self.send_message(
        message.sender,
        {"error": "Unsupported message type"},
        "error"
    )

async def perform_task(self, task: Dict[str, Any]) -> Dict[str, Any]:
    """Implementation of integration task execution"""
    self.log.info(f"Performing integration task: {task}")
    # Combine all available information into a coherent response
    response = await self.model.ainvoke([
        HumanMessage(content=f"Integrate these findings into a comprehensive
report: {json.dumps(task, indent=2)}")
    ])
    return {"integrated_response": response.content}
```

Explanation

- **Initialization**: Each agent is initialized with an ID, an LLM model instance, and a default state.
- **Abstract Methods**: *process_message* and *perform_task* are declared as abstract methods, ensuring that each specialized agent implements its own logic.
- ***send_message* Method**: This helper method constructs and logs a message to be sent to another agent.
- The **Coordinator Agent** orchestrates the overall process by receiving a high-level task, breaking it down into subtasks, and delegating these subtasks to other agents.
    - **process_message**: When the coordinator receives a *"task_request"*, it decomposes the task into subtasks for the researcher, analyst, and integrator.

- **perform_task**: This method creates a predefined set of subtasks. In a production system, this could be replaced with dynamic task decomposition logic.

- The **Research Agent** handles information gathering. It responds to research requests by invoking the LLM to gather data on a given topic.
  - **process_message**: Listens for *"research_request"* messages and, upon receipt, processes the task using the DeepSeek LLM.
  - **perform_task**: Uses the LLM to fetch research findings on the provided topic, then passes the results to the Integration Agent.
- The **Analysis Agent** is responsible for processing data and performing analytical calculations.
  - **process_message:** Catches *"analysis_request"* messages and processes them.
  - **perform_task:** Invokes the DeepSeek LLM to perform analysis on the given task and returns the resulting analysis.
- The **Integration Agent** combines outputs from the Research and Analysis agents into a final report. It stores intermediate results in its state and integrates them once all necessary data is available.
  - process_message:
    - For an *"integration_request"*, the agent immediately generates the final response.
    - For *"research_results"* or *"analysis_results"*, it stores the incoming data. Once both results are available, it integrates the findings.
  - perform_task: Uses the LLM to synthesize a comprehensive report from the aggregated data.

3. Creating the Multi-Agent System Manager

The *MultiAgentSystem* class orchestrates the entire process by initializing the agents, managing the message bus, and routing messages appropriately.

```
class MultiAgentSystem:
    def __init__(self):
        self.log = logging.getLogger("system")
        self.log.info("Initializing Multi-Agent System...")

        # Initialize LLM
        self.log.info("Creating LLM instance...")
        self.llm = ChatGroq(
            model="deepseek-r1-distill-llama-70b",
            temperature=0.6,
            max_tokens=2048
        )
```

```
        # Initialize agents
        self.log.info("Creating agents...")
        self.coordinator = CoordinatorAgent("coordinator", self.llm)
        self.researcher = ResearchAgent("researcher", self.llm)
        self.analyst = AnalysisAgent("analyst", self.llm)
        self.integrator = IntegrationAgent("integrator", self.llm)

        # Create agent registry
        self.agents = {
            "coordinator": self.coordinator,
            "researcher": self.researcher,
            "analyst": self.analyst,
            "integrator": self.integrator
        }

        # Initialize message bus
        self.log.info("Initializing message bus...")
        self.message_bus = asyncio.Queue()

    async def route_message(self, message: AgentMessage):
        """Route message to appropriate agent"""
        self.log.info(f"Routing message:\n{message}")

        if message.receiver in self.agents:
            receiver = self.agents[message.receiver]
            self.log.info(f"Found receiver: {message.receiver}")
            response = await receiver.process_message(message)
            if response:
                self.log.info(f"Received response from {message.receiver}")
                await self.message_bus.put(response)
        else:
            self.log.error(f"Unknown receiver: {message.receiver}")

    async def process_task(self, task: str) -> str:
        """Process task through multi-agent system"""
        self.log.info(f"Starting task processing:\n{task}")

        # Create initial task message
        initial_message = AgentMessage(
            sender="system",
            receiver="coordinator",
            message_type="task_request",
            content={"task": task},
            timestamp=datetime.now().isoformat(),
            priority=3,
            requires_response=True
        )

        # Start task processing
        self.log.info("Sending initial message to coordinator")
        await self.message_bus.put(initial_message)
```

```
        # Process messages until task completion
        while True:
            self.log.info("Waiting for next message...")
            message = await self.message_bus.get()
            self.log.info(f"Received message of type: {message.message_type}")

            if message.message_type == "final_response":
                self.log.info("Received final response")
                return message.content["response"]
            elif message.message_type == "error":
                self.log.error(f"Error received: {message.content['error']}")
                continue

            await self.route_message(message)
```

Explanation

- **Initialization**: The system creates an instance of the DeepSeek LLM and instantiates all four agents. Each agent is registered in a dictionary for easy routing.
- **Message Bus**: An *asyncio.Queue* serves as the central message bus that holds messages waiting to be processed.
- **Routing and Processing**: The *route_message* method forwards messages to the appropriate agent. The *process_task* method initiates the workflow by sending a task request to the Coordinator and then waits for a *"final_response"*.

3. Implementing Advanced Features

To further enhance the system, two advanced features are introduced: **Conflict Resolution** and **Knowledge Sharing**.

- Conflict Resolution
  The *ConflictResolver* class is designed to manage disagreements or conflicting outputs from different agents.
- Knowledge Sharing
  The KnowledgeBase class allows agents to share information through a centralized, concurrency-controlled repository.

```
### Conflict Resolution
class ConflictResolver:
    """Handles disagreements between agents"""
    def __init__(self, llm: ChatGroq):
        self.llm = llm

    async def resolve_conflict(self, messages: List[AgentMessage]) -> AgentMessage:
        """Analyze conflicting messages and determine resolution"""
        # Implementation details...
```

~~~
```

### Knowledge Sharing
class KnowledgeBase:
    """Shared knowledge repository for agents"""
    def __init__(self):
        self.knowledge = {}
        self._lock = asyncio.Lock()

    async def add_knowledge(self, key: str, value: Any):
        """Add new knowledge with concurrency control"""
        async with self._lock:
            self.knowledge[key] = value

    async def get_knowledge(self, key: str) -> Any:
        """Retrieve knowledge"""
        return self.knowledge.get(key)
~~~

Explanation

- **ConflictResolver**: Although the implementation details are omitted here, this class would analyze conflicting messages and use the LLM to suggest resolutions.
- **KnowledgeBase**: Implements a thread-safe (using an asynchronous lock) shared repository so that agents can read from and write to a common source of knowledge.

4. Example Usage

Below is an example of how to run the system. The main function sets up the multi-agent system, submits a complex task, and displays the final integrated response. Additionally, a *SystemMonitor* class is provided for performance tracking.

```
async def main():
    # Set up logging for main
    log = logging.getLogger("main")

    # Initialize system
    log.info("Creating Multi-Agent System...")
    system = MultiAgentSystem()

    # Create system monitor
    monitor = SystemMonitor()

    # Process complex task
    task = """
    Research the impact of artificial intelligence on healthcare,
    analyze the findings, and provide a comprehensive report with
    supporting data and recommendations.
    """
```

```
    log.info("Starting task processing...")

    try:
        response = await system.process_task(task)
        log.info("Task completed successfully")
        console.print("\n[bold green]Final Response:[/bold green]")
        console.print(response)
    except Exception as e:
        log.error(f"Error occurred: {str(e)}", exc_info=True)
        console.print_exception()

if __name__ == "__main__":
    console.print("[bold blue]Starting Multi-Agent System...[/bold blue]")
    asyncio.run(main())
```

6. Performance Monitoring and Optimization

```
class SystemMonitor:
    def __init__(self):
        self.log = logging.getLogger("monitor")
        self.start_time = datetime.now()
        self.message_count = 0
        self.error_count = 0

    def log_message(self, message: AgentMessage):
        self.message_count += 1
        if message.message_type == "error":
            self.error_count += 1

        elapsed = datetime.now() - self.start_time
        self.log.info(f"""
System Metrics:
- Runtime: {elapsed}
- Messages Processed: {self.message_count}
- Error Rate: {self.error_count/self.message_count:.2%}
""")
```

Explanation

- **main() Function**: Demonstrates the setup and execution of a complex task. The system processes the task by routing messages among agents until a final integrated response is produced.
- **SystemMonitor**: Tracks runtime metrics such as the number of messages processed and the error rate, helping to identify performance bottlenecks.

Conclusion

This implementation of a multi-agent system demonstrates how specialized agents can work together to solve complex problems. The system's modular design allows for easy extension and customization, while the structured communication protocol ensures reliable inter-agent coordination.

Key advantages of this approach include:
- Parallel processing of subtasks
- Specialized expertise for different aspects of complex problems
- Robust error handling and conflict resolution
- Scalable architecture for adding new agent types
- Comprehensive monitoring and optimization capabilities

For further development, consider:
- Adding more specialized agent types
- Implementing more sophisticated conflict resolution strategies
- Enhancing the knowledge sharing system
- Developing more advanced performance monitoring tools

Chapter 10: The Future of AI Reasoning

As we conclude our journey through DeepSeek R1 and its capabilities, we stand at an inflection point in the history of artificial intelligence. Throughout this book, we've explored how DeepSeek R1 represents a fundamental shift in AI development – not just in its technical capabilities, but in its approach to open-source collaboration and cost-effective deployment. Let's reflect on what we've learned and look ahead to what the future might hold.

The DeepSeek R1 Revolution

When DeepSeek emerged from Hangzhou in 2023, few could have predicted its impact on the AI landscape. Yet, by challenging the conventional wisdom that advanced AI requires massive resources and proprietary systems, DeepSeek R1 has demonstrated that sophisticated reasoning capabilities can be both accessible and affordable.

We've seen throughout this book how DeepSeek R1's architecture enables remarkable reasoning abilities while maintaining efficiency. From the mathematical prowess demonstrated in early chapters to the complex multi-agent systems we built in later sections, DeepSeek R1 has shown that open-source models can match or exceed the capabilities of their proprietary counterparts.

Key Lessons Learned

Our exploration has revealed several fundamental principles that will likely shape the future of AI development:

1. Reasoning as a First-Class Citizen
The success of DeepSeek R1 demonstrates that explicit reasoning capabilities should be central to AI system design, not merely an afterthought. We've seen how the model's architecture, training approach, and deployment strategies all work together to enable sophisticated problem-solving abilities.

2. The Power of Open Collaboration
DeepSeek's commitment to open-source development has created a virtuous cycle of innovation. As we discussed in earlier chapters, the ability for researchers and developers worldwide to examine, modify, and improve the model has accelerated its evolution in ways that closed systems cannot match.

3. Efficiency Through Design
The model's mixture-of-experts architecture and innovative training approaches show that efficiency needn't come at the cost of capability. This fundamental lesson will likely influence AI system design for years to come.

Looking to Tomorrow

As we look to the future, several exciting developments appear on the horizon:

Advanced Reasoning Architectures

The success of DeepSeek R1's reasoning capabilities points toward even more sophisticated architectures. We might expect to see:

- Integration of symbolic reasoning with neural approaches
- Enhanced logical inference capabilities
- More sophisticated multi-agent coordination systems
- Improved handling of uncertainty and ambiguity

Researchers are already exploring architectures that combine the strengths of neural networks with classical AI approaches to reasoning. These hybrid systems might offer the best of both worlds: the flexibility and learning capabilities of neural networks with the precision and reliability of symbolic systems.

Democratization of AI

DeepSeek's approach to open-source development and efficient deployment has implications far beyond any single model. We're likely to see:

- More accessible deployment options for small and medium enterprises
- Increased focus on resource-efficient architectures
- Greater emphasis on interpretability and explainability
- Expanded community-driven development efforts

This democratization of AI technology could lead to a proliferation of specialized models tailored to specific domains and use cases, each building on the foundational principles we've explored in this book.

Ethical Considerations and Responsible Development

As AI systems become more capable and widespread, the importance of ethical considerations grows. Future developments will likely focus on:

- Enhanced safety measures and guardrails
- Better bias detection and mitigation
- Improved transparency and accountability
- Stronger privacy protections and security measures

The open-source nature of DeepSeek R1 provides a valuable model for how these considerations can be addressed through community oversight and collaborative development.

Your Role in the Future of AI

As we conclude this book, it's worth considering your role in this evolving landscape. Whether you're a developer, researcher, or business leader, you now have the tools and understanding to contribute to the future of AI development.

Consider:

1. Building on the Fundamentals
The principles and practices we've covered provide a foundation for creating sophisticated AI systems. Use them as a starting point for your own innovations.

2. Contributing to the Community
The open-source nature of DeepSeek R1 means you can actively participate in its development. Share your improvements, report issues, and collaborate with others to advance the state of the art.

3. Pushing the Boundaries
Don't be afraid to experiment with new approaches and applications. The field is still young, and there's plenty of room for innovation.

Practical Next Steps

To continue your journey with DeepSeek R1 and AI development:

1. Join the Community
- Engage with the DeepSeek community on GitHub
- Participate in discussions and share your experiences
- Contribute to documentation and examples

2. Expand Your Knowledge
- Stay current with the latest research papers
- Experiment with different applications and use cases
- Share your findings with others

3. Build Real-World Applications
- Start with small projects and gradually increase complexity
- Focus on solving specific problems in your domain
- Document and share your successes and challenges

Final Thoughts

As we close this book, remember that we're still in the early stages of AI development. The principles and practices we've explored with DeepSeek R1 represent not an endpoint, but a beginning. The future of AI will be shaped by developers like you who take these foundations and build upon them.

The democratization of AI technology through models like DeepSeek R1 means that innovation can come from anywhere. Whether you're working at a large tech company or building something in your garage, you now have the tools and knowledge to contribute to this exciting field.

Keep exploring, keep building, and most importantly, keep sharing what you learn with others. The future of AI is open, and it belongs to all of us.

Resources for Continued Learning

Before we part ways, here are some valuable resources to support your ongoing journey:

1. Online Communities
- DeepSeek GitHub repository
- AI research forums and discussion groups
- Professional AI development communities

2. Technical Resources
- Research papers and technical documentation
- Code repositories and example projects
- Tutorial videos and workshops

3. Learning Platforms
- Online courses and tutorials
- Technical blogs and newsletters
- Conference presentations and workshops

Thank you for joining me on this exploration of DeepSeek R1 and the future of AI reasoning. I look forward to seeing what you'll build next.

Leave A Review

Thank you for reading this book.

I truly appreciate that you have taken the time to explore these pages. Your honest feedback is incredibly valuable—not only does it help other readers make informed decisions, but it also provides important insights that help me grow as a writer.

If you found this book meaningful or thought-provoking, I kindly invite you to share your experience by leaving a review on Amazon.

To do so, simply visit the book's product page on Amazon and scroll down to the customer review section, where you can click "Write a customer review."

https://www.amazon.com/review/create-review/?ie=UTF8&channel=glance-detail&asin=B0DWV75GWX

Your review can be as short or as detailed as you like; what matters most is your honest opinion. There is no expectation or requirement for a particular rating—please share what you truly think.

Thank you again for your support and for being a part of this journey. Every review helps me and future readers.

> If you'd like to stay updated on new releases, free resources, or events related to *The Complete AI Blueprint* series of books, please feel free to subscribe to our mailing list by sending an email to:
> James.karanja@zavora.ai

Warm Regards
James Karanja Maina